HANDS

—— WITHIN THE ——

BATTLE

MY MISSISSIPPI HISTORY

SECOND EDITION

MINNIE P. STEWART

ARPress
ILLUMINATING IDEAS.
EMPOWERING VOICES

ARPress
45 Dan Road Suite 5
Canton MA 02021

Hotline: 1(888) 821-0229
Fax: 1(508) 545-7580

Ordering Information:
Quantity sales. Special discounts are available on quantity purchases by corporations, associations, and others. For details, contact the publisher at the address above.

Printed in the United States of America.

ISBN-13:   Paperback   979-8-89356-279-8
              eBook   979-8-89356-278-1

Library of Congress Control Number: 2024903450

HANDS

WITHIN THE

BATTLE

Table of Contents

To my parents Lela Mae & Albert Smith;
the helping hands of our family.

A FIGHT FOR MAMA

Chapter 1

The phone rang with an unusual ring; it was as if sorrow was on the line. I quickly answered, and there it was-sorrow. My oldest sister, Bobbie Ann, was calling because of concerns for our mother. Mama wasn't eating right, wouldn't sleep in her bed, didn't want to take her medication, and was holding her urine for hours at a time. As Bobbie Ann was relaying the message to me, I could hear her voice change as she chocked up. In my mind I could see tears running down her checks. She cleared her throat and with a plea for help said, "What am I to do"? There I was on the other end of the line with no magical answer. After a short pause, I quickly said, "let me talk to Mama."

"Well hello Mama", I said. With a soft whisper of a voice she answered, "Hello Minnie". Getting straight to the point I asked, "What is this I am hearing about you not eating well, you not wanting to take you medication, not wanting to sleep in your bed; and why in the world would you want to hold your urine"? Mama softly explained that Bobbie Ann was exaggerating the matter. She slowly went on to explain her side of the story. After much conversation it was clear that she had what she considered a valid response to each item in question. To sum things up; Bobbie Ann's cooking was too salty, the walls of her room were closing in on her, her medication made her feel worst instead of better, and her legs hurt so bad that it was better to hold her urine and save her legs two or three unnecessary trips to the restroom.

What could I possibly do? Here I am almost eight hundred miles away with a family, a job and recovering from an illness myself. For Bobbie to call as she did there was a problem. Bobbie Ann knew if anyone could talk Mama into doing something, it would be me. I could sense that there was a real problem; I could feel it all through my body. My temples pulsated with pressure, my mouth watered, my stomach bubbled, and I broke out in a cold sweat. I had no chose but to talk about Mama's condition with my other sister, Albertine. After talking to Albertine I found out both were telling the truth as they saw it. For some reason I felt that there was more to this story. Why would a lady that's known for helping others to do the right thing for their own bodies, start neglecting her own. In the back of my mind I wondered, had my 81 year old mother given up on life. If she had, I was willing to fight to give it back to her.

To understand the reason for the fight for Mama's life is to know the life Mama lived. Mama was always giving of herself to others. She didn't have a lot of money to give, but she gave much service to those around her. Mama was one of only a few women in the neighborhood that didn't work, so she had the time to care for the sick and shut-ins in our community.

Not only did the community rely on Mama, old man Dr. Johnston did too. You see Mama even delivered a few babies in her days.

One day Mama had just finished cooking dinner when Jo Boy banged at the door saying, "Mrs. Smith, Mrs. Smith". As Mama was rushing to the door, Jo Boy pierced through the screen door saying, "Mommy is ready to have the baby. Dr. Johnston can't come right now, so he told my dad to send for you".

Mama checked the stove, grabbed her big brown purse, and locked the door, told us to come on that we knew how to act, as we rushed to Jo Boy's house. When we made it there, she said, "You girls sit here on the couch; we'll call Albert after 5 o'clock". We did just as she said. We knew why we were there, so we just sit back and listened to the radio. It seemed like such a long time.

Mama had been in the kitchen boiling water, as she went back and forth into the bathroom and bedroom. I knew she had everything she needed in her big brown purse including the scissors for cutting the cord, and lots of bleached flour sacks in a brown paper bag. I could smell the Lysol that comes in a little brown bottle, the good kind. I knew Lysol was in the bag too, because Mama had a thing about germs.

I couldn't help but wonder where the doctor was. I could hear Jo Boy's mother scream and moan. I just wanted to go outside; instead we had to sit in the living room with Jo Boy's father. Is this a joke-his kids are outside playing, and we are inside in misery. My mind was thinking of some of everything, and then I heard it-a baby's cry. I thought to myself, it's over. Boy was I wrong; it was about an hour before the afterbirth came.

Would you believe after everything was over, in came old Dr. Johnston. He said he was delivering another baby. All he could say was, "Miss Smith did a real good job. Did the afterbirth come?' This doctor did a quick check of the baby and was gone in less than 30 minutes. He even had the nerve to tell Jo Boy's dad to come by the office to set up payments. As always Mama never charged anything. Knowing Mama, she's going to cook a few meals for the family, and maybe sew a new outfit for the baby. As always, old Dr. Johnston never offered Mama a dollar for doing his job.

One time after helping a very sick mother deliver a baby girl, Mama vowed to keep the baby if the mother died. Mama kept that baby for two or three weeks until the grandmother was located. Mama was sad that she had to give the baby up; we were sad too because we enjoyed helping with the baby. Mama helped us to understand that this grandmother needed this baby to help cover the loss of her dead daughter. She will probably treat this baby better than she treated her own daughter. It's like this grandmother has been given another chance. Life is really something.

Mama, Lela Mae Smith, was only 5 ft 2 ins. tall, light brown skin with brown eyes. When I was a little girl Mama had a very small waist, but by the time I was in Junior high she had developed a thyroid problem that caused her to gain weight. I remember Mama having so much energy, that she was always doing something. She cooked all the time; breakfast, lunch and dinner. Several days a week before I started to school, I would walk with Mama to Dad's job at Avery Body Plant to take Dad a hot lunch. Mama made many of our school clothes without a pattern. I even remember Mama mentoring young women on moral issues, and on being a good wife and mother. Mama helped to raise five of my cousins, as well as helped with many neighborhood kids free of charge. She cooked the best molasses bread, tea cakes, and sweet bread you'll ever want to eat. Mama made sure she baked enough for kids of working mothers, so they would also have a snack after school. After school the aroma would fill the air as we walked toward the house. Our home was known as The Happy House.

A lot of what was work for Mama was sure fun for us girls. Early in the summer Mama walked about two miles with us to a place called The Rag Barn to buy left over boats of cloth. There was any and every color you could think of. The Rag Barn was a huge warehouse filled with table after table of left over fabrics from fashion houses where everything was sold by the pound. Twenty dollars would be enough money to buy fabrics to make four or five outfits each. Within a month we would be back again to buy more fabric.

I don't understand how Mama did it, but she looked in the Sears and Roebuck catalogue and made anything she wanted without a pattern. A matter of fact our clothes looked better than the catalogue, because Mama had a habit of making improvements on the catalogue clothes. Mama had a very organized system of doing things. Mama would pin and cut out a complete set of clothes from one type of fabric, while using various kinds of trim. Next, she would sew and fit the set. She would use nights or any sitting around time to do her hand sewing. When Mama was done, she would iron and hang the complete set of clothes up. It was unbelievable how Mama could take a plain piece of fabric and turn it into something so beautiful and perfect to ware. By early August, she would be done with all her sewing. Then we would buy socks and underclothes. Dad's job was to take us to buy our Buster Brown shoes, and to get our free egg filled with candy and a toy with each pair. Oh my, those were fun times.

Mama was really something. Mama feared drunk people, but still promised a dying mother that she would feed her drunkard partly disabled son after her death. As always, Mama kept her promise by feeding Abby. Abby was our neighborhood drunk that was shell shot, and had other medical problems. Mama was so afraid of drunken Abby that she made us fearful of drunks too. If I saw Abby coming I would start running into the house screaming, "Abby is coming, Abby is coming". We would run inside and lock the door. No matter how drunk Abby was, he knew to come to our house for his dinner. Mama would tell Abby to step away from the porch, as she placed his food on a bench on the porch. After the food was placed on the porch, Abby would get his food and start singing as he walked down the path to the next street. As we pierced out of the picture window, we could see Abby stagger down the path. When he was completely out of sight, we were allowed to go outside again.

Abby was one of the luckiest drunks in town. Not only did he get his food on time, he ate well. Mama cooked big meals every day. Just thinking about it makes me hungry. I can just taste the greens, peas, lima beans, cornbread, chicken and dumpling, candied yams, macaroni and cheese, rice with gravy, catfish, pork chops, fried green tomatoes, fried okra, any cake you can name, pies, cobblers cookies-Oh My. Almost every Sunday there was hen and dressing, or roast beef, or something like that. Abby had it made because Mama kept her promise to a dying mother until Abby took seriously ill, and moved with relatives out of town. For over two years Mama kept her promise, and never took a penny for her services.

Mama's unconditional love was on a higher level. She never expected anything in return for her love, concern or service. She went out of her way to make everyone feel worthwhile. I remember one summer day when I was around five or six; I picked a beautiful bunch of yellow flowers. I ran into the house to give them to Mama. She gave me a big hug and smile. Mama thanked me for the flowers as she put them in her prettiest jelly jar.

She proudly placed them on the window seal, and gave me a smile that was worth a million dollars. She never once said my beautiful yellow flowers were dandelions. Instead, she said they were the most beautiful yellow flowers she had ever seen.

I've learned so much by just being around Mama. I've learned to put family and others before myself. I've learned that it is more blessed to give than to receive. I've learned the necessary skills to be a good mother and wife. But most of all I've learned about unconditional love, because I was loved unconditionally by Mama. You see, with all I've gained, it's no more than right for me to help Mama fight to regain her spark for life.

GROWING UP IN MISSISSIPPI

Chapter 2

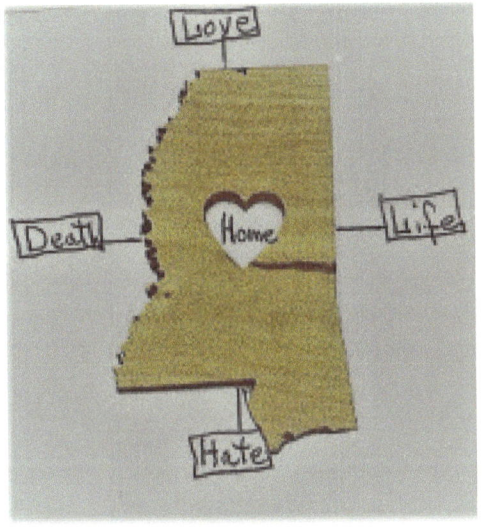

I've heard many people say bad things about growing up in Mississippi. As I look back at my Mississippi life, and having experienced thirty years of looking at my children grow up in Illinois; I must say I disagree. There are good and bad points to any place you live, depending on what you are looking for, and what you intend to gain.

Growing up in Mississippi has given me a body of knowledge, and experiences that I find hard to share. Some of my experiences bring tears to my eyes; these are not always sad tears, but many are happy deep appreciative tears of joy. I've heard it said, that one should just pour out your feeling so others will understand you. How can one just pour out personal feelings to someone that might not care, or understand where your feelings are coming from? To help you understand my feelings and concern for Mama, I need you to understand a little about me.

I surprise myself sometimes. I don't know why I am drawn to the needy, mistreated, friendless, or seasoned with time person. I don't know why I enjoy looking at insects busy at work and play, enjoy the smell of rain, can find endless beauty in a clover patch, can listen to birds sing and join in with them, or why I look around for hours at the beauty of the earth and find something amazing each time. I don't know why I can look at a newborn baby, or an elderly couple holding hands and get chocked up inside. I don't know why I'll rather receive a card with words of deep meaning, than one filled with money. I don't know why I enjoy the simple things in life. I just keep telling myself that this is just the way I am; only God truly knows.

I know Mama and Daddy are partly responsible for my inner feelings, but also my experiences of growing up in Mississippi. I've lived through the "Whites Only" and "Colored Only" signs, colored and white schools, civil rights marches, freedom riders, assassinations, integration and racial healing. Growing up in Mississippi has made me a better not bitter, stronger not weaker person. By God putting me in the right hands, the battle forces of inequality didn't break me.

My parents have helped me to become a strong, caring, giving Christian woman. I think of life like a maze. How we travel through this maze determines our life's outcome. Who we are, and what we will become is like traveling through this maze of life. At many points in life there will be choices to make that will determine the next path in life. Some choices will lead down paths that will lead to rewards or gratifications; others will lead to detours, disappointments and destruction. To some degree we are given guides to help guide us through this maze of life. If we listen; we may be able to avoid many detours, disappointments or even destruction. God blessed me with five such people; my mother, father, grandmother, grandfather, and godmother. My parents were both strong beautiful people inside and outside. Their value system was based on Christian values, wisdom and the golden rule.

My grandparents were also truly inspirational. I've been told that I look so much like my grandmother, that I was named after her. It seemed like Grandma favored me a little too. I always wanted to know how to do things, and how things worked. For a little girl I enjoyed being in the kitchen. Grandma showed me how to make her buttermilk biscuits. She started me out standing on a step stool and letting me cut them out, and also shaping them by hand. I would have flour on the floor, the table and on me. I had a chance to help cook and sample all kinds of foods before they were ready to be served.

During the summer we girls would visit our grandparents for two weeks. We would have so much fun, and get in so much trouble. Us four girls would tire our grandparents out so; they would be happy to see us arrive, and even happier to see us leave.

There were other people living in our grandparent's big house. We were told that when our aunts divorced they moved back home. There was Aunt Thelma and her son Curtis; we called him Little Boy. There was also Mama's oldest sister Aunt Eva and her son Freddie; we called him Shug. I never knew how to place my Uncle Jack. To me he wasn't like an uncle, because he was just a few years older than my cousins. Jack was the youngest of ten kids; seven girls and three boys.

We would let Little Boy and Shug make utter fools out of us. They knew the rules; but would let, or even tell us what to do to break the rules. We would jump from the loft of a barn onto a wagon filled with hay. We tried to catch, and ride pigs. You can imagine what we smelled like. We tried to catch banty chicks, to later find out that the hen would attack us. We stole watermelons from the watermelon patch. Bobbie Ann even pulled green pecan from a pecan tree to eat. Little Boy and Shug told her that she had to bite the green shell off first. That's exactly what she did. For three months Bobbie Ann had green teeth. One day after watching Little Boy and Shug milk the cows, I ask them to give me just one cup of fresh milk. They told me that I had to get my own. I wiped off a tit and did just that until my stomach was full. Boy did Little Boy and Shug get in trouble for that prank. I felt like I was punished for my cousins letting me do wrong. Grandma was so afraid that I would get worms that she decided to de-worm me with castor oil. For the rest of the day I ran back and forth to the outhouse

Poor Bobbie Ann decided to sample some of Grandpa's chewing tobacco. Bobbie Ann's biggest problem was swallowing instead of spitting the liquid out, believe it or not, Bobbie Ann was sicker than I was. We spent a lot of time in the outhouse that day. This outhouse had two potty holes; there was no waiting in line. To keep from going back and forth, we decided to stay in the outhouse for long periods of time just sitting, talking or using it. Grandma made it clear that we couldn't ware those "fancy dresses" on the farm. Grandpa wanted us to fit in, so he bought us overalls with buttons on the butt for using the outhouse. We might have looked the part, but we never fit in.

When we wanted to pick cotton, Grandma made us cotton picking sacks out of large flour sack. I tried to pick cotton, and it wasn't easy or fun. At the age of nine I had such a hard time trying to fill my sack that I decided to steal cotton from Aunt Thelma and Aunt Eva's cotton sacks. I don't know how they picked cotton so fast. Every time I turn around they were taking their sacks to be weighted. These women were picking hundreds of pounds of cotton a day. Surely they wouldn't miss a few handfuls of cotton. I soon learned that it didn't pay to steal cotton. For all my hard work and stealing cotton, I only made thirty five cents for the whole day. Really, riding on Aunt Thelma's sack, and eating watermelons along the cotton field was more fun. Grandpa got upset and said, "picking cotton was a job, not a game". As you can imagine, I gladly quit that job. The next day my other sisters quit too. It was more fun spending time with Grandma doing fun things in the kitchen, and around the house. We had to constantly clean, wash clothes, and cook. Grandma loved for me to work with her, because I loved to work. Grandma taught me how to churn milk to make butter; how to pick and prepare vegetables from the garden. At nine I learned how to cook pancakes, sweetbread, and even cornbread.

Learning from my godmother was a true adventure. Ms. Sister, as we called her, was a true Native American. Ms. Sister taught me to love and respect nature. I remember one time she killed a four feet king snake. I had never seen anything like that before, nor since. The snake was put across the gate, where its tail just dangled for about an hour. She explained how the king snake was important because it killed other harmful snakes and rodents. This snake had to be killed, because it decided to make its home underneath her home. She couldn't share her home with a snake. Ms. Sister hated to kill the snake, but she didn't want her home to become snake invested.

Going next door to visit Ms. Sister was an adventure. There was an old fashioned swing that hung from an old shady oak tree. There were also two of the tallest fig trees I had ever seen. At the top of the trees were many bird nests. The birds would eat from the top of the trees, and we would eat from the rest of the trees. There was always something to do, or old Indian stories to listen to. A many days we would just sit on a long enclosed porch lined with rocking chairs, and talk. Ms. Sister would share stories about her Indian childhood, and about how her family had been mistreated. Ms. Sister would always talk about nature, and how I had to respect nature and all of God's creatures.

Also next door was Mr. George, Ms. Kathy and sneaky Georgie. Mr. George was my godfather, but he didn't talk much. I mainly remember him bringing me typing paper from the paper mill factory where he worked. I was the only kid in the neighborhood walking around with typing paper. Boy did I have fun playing teacher, and giving out typing paper. Ms. Kathy was my godmother's sister-in-law, and Georgie's grandmother. I didn't think Kathy really liked me; so I showered her with love anyway. I finally won her over, but she just didn't want to show it. A many times I would feel that Ms. Kathy was laughing or smiling at me; only to turn around to see her cut her laughing or smile off. I had a habit of singing and dancing, reciting things I had learned at school or church, or showing off all the wonderful things I was doing with my typing paper. Ms. Kathy knew I was one smart girl that showed and received love from Ms. Sister. Maybe I was the outsider getting the attention Georgie could have been getting from my godparents.

Jackson, Mississippi's colored schools were lacking in some of its materials, but the great teachers made up for it. The white kids we talked to, and played with couldn't understand how we got so smart. We could read well, write well, speak well, and do math with great speed. For some reason the white parents though we shouldn't read, write, or do math well. With all the typing paper I had, I proved them wrong as I played teacher. I found out at a young age that white parents didn't like for "colored" kids to teach their kids anything related to reading, writing or math.

One day as Dad was cutting Mrs. Carmichael's yard, I was playing school with her daughter Elizabeth. Elizabeth was having problems with her time tables. I was teaching Elizabeth a fun way to learn her time tables.

We were having fun and learning too. I had just taught Elizabeth my secret to doing times tables, and hopscotch at the same time. Mrs. Carmichael heard us and got very upset; and had Elizabeth to come inside. As Mrs. Carmichael pulled her inside the door, she was shouting at the top of her voice. I heard her shout, 'That nigger can't teach you; they don't know nothing. Don't you ever let no little nigger teach you". That day Mrs. Carmichael made it clear what she felt about me.

It would really hurt Mrs. Carmichael to find out that I did become a teacher. She would probable pass out to know that my name is forever written in Who's Who Among America's Teachers for years 1996 and 1998; not to mention the first Black high school teacher in Rockford, Illinois to win the Golden Apple Teachers Award (1998). I could really tell Mrs. Carmichael a few things. What I really would like to know is, where is Elizabeth and what is she doing now? When I was at Jackson State College, Elizabeth was working at Sears and Roebucks full time. Her mother might have not understood our friendship, but we knew it was an unconditional nonjudgmental friendship. We were two little girls having fun. It seems odd for me to say this, but I do miss my friend. Our friendship ended too soon, and for the wrong reason.

Growing up in Mississippi has given me a chance to see racial attitudes change. I saw White Only and Colored signs. I experienced segregation in schools, stores, restaurants, work places, and common everyday places. I experienced seeing people hurt, or killed for speaking out about racial injustice. It was hard to understand how the color of one's skin or even race could determine one's life value. I am so happy that Mom and Dad made it clear that the problem wasn't us; it was the insecurities and fears of whites. It was made clear that some prejudice attitudes can never change, and that some prejudice people already know the truth. Their mission in life is keeping others from finding out the truth too. Our mission as a Black race is to make sure that the truth be made know. The best way to change attitudes is to prove that these prejudice attitudes don't have true bases. Dad said that we had to be better than the best. We have to learn all that we can, be the best worker on the job, and learn that "Silence Is Golden". We need to know when to speak out, how much to reveal, and to whom to reveal it to. In some cases a "colored" knowing too much can be a scary thing to a poor, uneducated or prejudice white person. Part of this prejudice attitude is learned, the rest is based on fear of the unknown. As Dad put it, "We don't want to take anything from anybody, we just want the right to earn our own. This is why the best is so important. Maybe the right person will see your hard work, and give you a chance to prove yourself. If this ever happens, it's time to show what you know; as well as let others know you are eager, willing, and able to learn more to be the best at that job."

Dad didn't tell us to do anything that he couldn't or wouldn't do himself. Dad confronted his boss, Mr. Avery about the injustice he showed toward him. Dad helped Mr. Avery with plant equipment problems, as well as trained new workers. Mr. Avery even had Dad to speak to some of the Black workers during plant meetings. Dad even went to Mr. Avery with complaints from Black workers. The problem came when Mr. Avery hired a young White man. Mr. Avery had Dad to train this man, and within months this young "white boy", as Dad called him; became Dad's supervisor. I didn't hear the conversation at the plant, but I did her the conversation in our home.

Plant meeting with Mr. Avery
(Dad is in the 3rd frame; bottom corner, fist person)

When Dad made it home from work he was very upset. No, he was mad. Mom said, "Albert you need to talk to Mr. Avery; just the two of you. You know he doesn't want people to know how you really talk back to him". "I guess you are right. But, he really hurt me this time Sister. I am going to stop helping him out so much", said Dad. Mom used Dad's own words on him, "Pray about it".

After dinner Dad received a call from Mr. Avery. I don't know what Mr. Avery said to Dad; all I know was Dad said, "You can come over". Mom put on a pot of coffee as Dad waited. It wasn't long before Mr. Avery was pulling up in the yard. Mom had us girls to go in the bedroom. Dad got loud with Mr. Avery, and Mr. Avery got loud with Dad too. After a few minutes things were all quiet. Mom came to the bedroom to see did we want cake and milk. As always we had to go to the table to eat. I couldn't believe what I had heard; Mr. Avery said, "Albert I am sorry, I'll make it right". I didn't hear Dad say anything. Soon Dad walked Mr. Avery to the door, and they said goodbye to each other.

Mr. Avery did make some changes. Dad no longer had a supervisor; he only answered to Mr. Avery. Dad didn't get a raise, but he got something better. Mr. Avery started bringing more things to the house. The most surprising thing happened around the 4th of July. Mr. Avery gave all workers around five bow dollars (silver coins) for the 4th of July. What was really different; Mr. Avery came by the house, and had all four of us girls come to the living room. He gave each of us a bow dollar. He gave Mama and Daddy five bow dollars each. He had Daddy and us girls o go to the car with him. He gave us bags of meat, fruit and even sweet potatoes. As Dad thanked Mr. Avery; Mr. Avery said, "I told you I'll make it right". Dad said, "Yes, thank you". Mr. Avery kept his word; he continued to come by before Thanksgiving, Christmas, Labor Day and the 4th of July. The strangest thing to us girls was Mr. Avery gave us one additional bow dollar each year. Mr. Avery was Dad's friend. The saddest thing was, he didn't want his White friends to know. What kind of friend was that?

I had a chance to experience the integration process, although Dad had already exposed us to it. At Sears and Roebuck, and Liberty Super Market; Dad would stand by us as we would drink from the cool "Whites Only" water fountain. Dad dressed nice, knew how to talk to people, and he didn't play. It was surprising how many whites called Dad "Mr. Smith or

Albert". I never heard anybody call Dad "boy or ha you". We were taught to look directly in the eyes of a person when you talked to them. Eyes reveal the real person and their real feelings. Growing up I really didn't think this information was so important. In Mississippi many whites made it clear that they didn't like coloreds. It wasn't until I moved to Illinois that I had to relearn the lesson that eyes reveal the true person and their true feeling. For the last forty six years I've made it a point of reading people through their eyes. I must say that Dad was right, and I've read people right about ninety percent of the time. I also found out that this rule doesn't apply to very shy people. Shy people will lose it, and think you're out to get them if you constantly stare in their eyes.

I did experience a lot of hurt and sorrow in Mississippi, but the love I experienced far outweighed the hurt and sorrow. As I look back, I realize that the hurt and sorrow that I experienced was experienced by people throughout the U.S. I can't begin to express the hurt I felt during the sixties when Medgar Evers, President John F. Kennedy and Dr. Martin Luther King, Jr. were assassinated. At that time, there was so much fear and uncertainty about the future as we heard about missing and killed Freedom Riders.

The Black community started having more and more civil rights meeting in homes, churches, and almost anywhere there was space for a meeting. Most information about meetings was passed along by word of mouth or through Black churches. High school students were speaking out more, and becoming fired up by the Freedom Riders that were showing up at our meetings. Secretly, Freedom Riders were in Black and White homes in surrounding areas from Jackson to Canton, MS. Freedom Riders were coming in and out of Jackson, and the police didn't even know it. The police were so busy arresting Freedom Riders coming in on Greyhound and Trailways buses; that they didn't know many were coming into Jackson on two lanes Highway 51. Highway 51 is a two lanes road that went through small towns and farm land. People were coming and going in plain cars and pickup trucks.

In the spring of 1963 even Dr. King came to speak in our neighborhood at St. Matthews M.B. church at the corner of Fontaine Ave. and Rockdale Dr. Dr. King was in and out of town before the police knew he was even in town. It was because of this meeting and other meeting like it that Barbara

Nell and Bobbie Ann took part in the civil rights movement. Barbara Nell started voicing her opinion, and was an active member of Sam M. Brinkley High School's Journalism Club. That spring Barbara Nell and Bobbie Ann took part in a protest march with other high school students from Lanier, Sam M. Brinkley, and Jim Hill High Schools. As Freedom Riders and community leaders met, it was decided to boycott businesses on downtown Capital Street. This boycott was during the Easter season, and it hit white businesses very hard. Old and young alike went along with the boycott and some whites too. As more riders came into Jackson on buses, they were quickly arrested for trying to use segregated restrooms at the terminals. Teenagers and neighborhood groups made signs, and started picking downtown Jackson on Capital Street.

On the news [WLBT (NBC), WAPT (ABC), and WJTV (CBS); spring 1963] it was reported that the crowds were in the hundreds. Whites were fussing, calling the picketers niggers and nigger lovers. My parents were very afraid for Barbara Nell and Bobbie Ann. They became more afraid as they saw picketers being tossed about and knocked down from the forceful water of fire hoses. It was so painful to see people loaded into paddy wagons and garbage trucks. A short glance of the fairgrounds with people packed into stockades sent a real message for all of America to see.

There were so many arrests that day that they ran out of buses, paddy wagons, and garbage trucks to load people into. As the group got smaller, Bobbie Ann couldn't find Barbara Nell. As Bobbie Ann ran looking near the loaded buses she saw several people she knew. As the buses started to pull off, all Bobbie Ann could see were crying, screaming, and singing faces. On the second bus pulling off was Barbara Nell. Her face was pressed against the window of the crowded bus. All Bobbie Ann could see were Barbara Nell's big brown eyes staring at her. Bobbie Ann stopped, and just stared back. There was nothing she could do, nothing at all.

As the group got smaller, Bobbie Ann started walking toward a safe area near Farish Street. Farish Street a historic Black strip of Black owned businesses including the famous Alamo Theater and Peaches Restaurant. There were other teens there trying to decide what to do next. Bobbie Ann's group knew they needed to start walking home. How could Bobbie Ann go home without Barbara Nell? What could she tell Mama and Daddy? She knew she had to tell the truth.

As Bobbie Ann walked through the door, she quickly sat on the couch. She really looked bad and scared; like she had been to hell and back. All Mama could say was, "Where is Barbara Nell, where is Barbara Nell. Oh no!! " "Mama, Barbara Nell is going to be okay", said Bobbie Ann. Then another report came over the news that hundreds of people were arrested, and wouldn't be released today. The news showed livestock stockades where people were just packed in. The same news was on all the major channels and the radio too. Many people in other states probably had no idea what a stockade was. In many southern states we knew stockades as dirty livestock cages used for storing livestock for transporting. Yes, these were smelly dirty livestock cages. The way the protesters were treated sent the message throughout America that Mississippi will stop protesters even if they have to enslave them. This news showed that, "once again we were caged and mad".

Bobbie Ann moved to the edge of the couch as she explained how they got separated. Bobbie Ann told how they were hosed, knocked down, and how she flipped over and over on the ground from the pressure of the water. When she got up they were separated. She started to look for her, as police started to load people in paddy wagons, on buses, and even garbage trucks. People started running up side streets, and even back down Capital Street away from the Capital building. As buses started to leave she saw Barbara Nell on the second bus. She looked scared, but she was okay. Daddy looked at Bobbie Ann and said, "Why didn't you get arrest?" Bobbie Ann paused and said, "They ran out of buses and places to put us." Mama took Bobbie Ann to the bathroom as she said, "Let's get you cleaned up."

It appeared that there was a hidden agenda to kill everyone that took a leadership role in the Civil Rights Movement. Medgar Evers, our area NAACP leader, was shot dead in front of his home on June 11, 1963. I remember it well. I was just turning fifteen with a feeling I couldn't label; was it fear or was it hate? How could someone come into our neighborhood and take the life of a man with so much vision and hope?

Just two months later Dr. King delivered a speech that brought the Civil Rights Movement to the front and center of public attention. On August 28, 1963 Dr. King delivered his "I Have A Dream Today" speech before a quarter of a million people at the Lincoln Memorial (WJTV;

August 28-30, 1963). I had never heard such a speech like this in my life. Dr. King's words were so powerful and direct, not to mention moving. To this point in my life, I still consider Dr. King's speech the greatest speech I've ever heard given. Also during this time President Kennedy was working on the Civil Rights Act; that would give equal rights to all people, Black and White alike. There was a vision and hope after all.

On November 22, 1963 just five months after Medgar Evers was killed, I heard the news that President John F. Kennedy had been shot. I remember it as if it happened today. An announcement was made over the intercom system at Sam M. Brinkley High School, "President Kennedy has been shot, and he has died."

Everybody started screaming and crying, including my teacher. Students ran outside and kneeled down at the flag pole and just cried, prayed, and sang freedom and gospel songs. To this day, I don't know what time I made it home, or even remember walking home. So much hope was lost with the death of President Kennedy, and not knowing whether Vice President Johnson would have the same vision. We were losing years of progress, and gaining added fear of the future. What God has for you, no man can take away. On July 2, 1964 President Lyndon B. Johnson signed into law the Civil Rights Act, as Dr. Martin Luther King, Jr. looked on witnessing this great moment in history (WJTV; July 2-4, 1964). Saturday July 4, 1964 was a celebration in Jackson like nothing I had ever seen. Farish Street was packed and music was everywhere. Our neighborhood smelled like barbeque and we could hear music from everywhere. Kids were riding bikes in the street, playing street ball, people were barbequing in the front yard, and teens were grouped together talking and all around were red, white, and blue. This was new to me because we always visited my grandparents for the 4th. This time we were afraid to travel through Brandon because it was known as KKK territory, so Mama decided not to go to Fannin to our yearly July 4th family picnic. It really didn't matter, I was having fun.

Emotions were high as more Whites started to show up in the neighborhood, at churches, and at meetings. More Whites were beginning to see and understand the struggle of Blacks. During this time Malcolm X emphasized Black Power, as James Brown sang "I Am Black and I Am Proud".

Dr. King began to speak out more and more. There were boycotts, freedom marches, voter registration drives, sit-ins and freedom rallies. A march that is still engraved in my brain was June 26, 1966. I remember it well because it was right after graduation and down Bailey Ave. just behind our home. The march started at Tugaloo College, and was to end on the steps of the Capital Building. Many people gathered on both sides of Bailey Ave. hoping to get a glimpse of Dr. King and even join in the march. Mama stayed inside our backyard fence, while Dad walked out to Bailey Ave. with Albertine and me. For some reason a group of neighborhood teenagers grouped around us. Dad explained to the group that he didn't want them to go, but he understood why they had to march. Dad talked about being safe and staying together. As they formed a circle, Dad prayed for the group, Dr. King, and all those that were taking part in the march.

I wanted to march so badly, but Mom and Dad felt Albertine and I was not emotionally ready to handle what might happen to us. They didn't want us to experience the hatred Bobbie Ann and Barbara Nell had experienced in 1963. Also, they didn't want anything to happen that would interfere with me going to college in August.

As the marchers got closer, we could hear them before we could see them. Oh my, there were National Guard men on a huge military truck, and hundreds of people behind. Dad shook his head with his mouth open, but no words came out. Leading the marchers were Dr. King, Stokely Carmichael, Floyd McKissick, and many other people we knew weren't from Jackson. This was a sight to behold. The singing, waving, clapping, crying, and signs made this bigger than any parade I had even seemed. People along the side of Bailey Ave. joined in as the group Dad prayed for did the same. I was just thinking, where did all these people come from? Young whites, old whites, all shades and ages of Black people, and some people that I couldn't identify by race. All of these people identified with a part of Dr. King's great speech; I Have A Dream Today. A ways back was another National Guards truck.

The march did end at the Capital Building, but instead of a powerful rally, there was a powerful resistive force. White people and police officers lined Capital Street, and the steps to the Capital Building. Marchers continued to march to the state Capital Building. The resistance was Whites shouting, "Niggers go home" and "Nigger lovers". Marchers were hosed, arrested, and packed onto paddy wagons and buses. That day hundreds of people were arrested. Marchers were loaded onto buses, and taken to be packed into livestock stockades like cattle just like before. Only this time reporters had come into Jackson from many other states. This was history in the making. Marchers were held overnight and released later the next day (WJTV; June 26-28, 1966).

Mississippi sent American another message that, "We'll stop you even if we have to enslave you". The news showed people being hosed, tossed about, arrested and packed into stockades. Once again, we are "caged and mad".

After the Civil Rights March of 1966; it felt like things were getting better. Jackson State College Black Pride filled the air. The Civil Rights movement was moving in the right direction. Dr. King was speaking more, voter registration was moving forth, and integration appeared to be working. With Dr. King, the NAACP, and Black pride moving throughout the Unites States; we became more of a treat than ever before. We knew it and Whites did too. I couldn't help but think of how so many people had given their lives for this movement. I had heard the rumor, but wouldn't say it, and I definitely tried not to think it. No, I won't pass this rumor around. All I could do was pray for God to protect and keep him safe.

Mama's 50th birthday was Tuesday April 2, 1968. We had showered her with gifts, good food and family. We had decided to have a big family and friend's dinner on the weekend. The week was going great, but on Thursday a news flash came on in the middle of our evening story. The new flash stated that Dr. Martin Luther King Jr. was shot at 6:05 P.M. on the balcony of his second floor room in Memphis, TN. After watching the continuous news flashes, and waiting; it was later announced that Dr. Martin Luther King Jr. died at 7:05 P.M. (WJTV; April 4, 1968). This news was on all the channels. How could this be happening again? When will it ever stop? The rumor was right; Whites were going to do everything they could to stop Dr. King. Sure he has been killed, but his message will never die. As a People we must always keep Dr. King's message alive. We must fight to keep his dream alive.

Growing up in Mississippi has taught me to value contributions of my forefathers. I've learned to do my best at every opportunity I've been given. I've kept in mind that many opportunities in life were made possible because of sacrifices and struggles of others. As I discussed my feelings and what I know about the Civil Rights Movement with my sisters a new fear rose up in me. What I thought was a new movement for youth protestors wasn't new at all. Dernoral Davis did a feature story about youth protestors in the movement. The story covered 1955 to 1970 (Davis; 2000). That means I was only seven years old when this movement started, and covers up to me graduating from college. This feature story confirmed my sister experiences within the movement. Best yet; I had living witnesses and my own experiences that I needed to document and share with our off springs, Wow, we are "Living History".

When I talk of my Mississippi experiences, people don't believe I didn't have to sit at the back of the bus. When we lived under the hill we didn't use a city bus, we walked where we wanted to go, ride in a neighbor's car or take our neighborhood taxi. I started using the city bus when we moved to Cottage Grove at the age of twelve. We had our own bus, if a white got on the bus they had to sit on any vacant seat. No one gave up their seat. As teenagers we took the city bus to shop downtown, go to the movies, go to Jackson State College, or other Black subdivisions.

The whites were so busy making sure we were separated from them; that unbeknown to them they created a way for us to become more independent. During the boycotts we had almost everything we needed in our own neighborhoods. We always knew how to share, and live within our means. Most families taught their kids to cook, I mean really cook. By kids knowing how to cook, it was away of passing down survival skills. Black kids weren't bored during the boycotts because they were busy helping to cook, do chores, playing and fellowshipping with other kids. A lot of chickens were killed when we were going through boycotts. We were taught to bake, fry, stew, roast, smother, make chicken soup, chicken and dumpling, chicken and dressing, chicken pot pie, and make chicken surprise. Chicken surprise was like dump pot; where you use refrigerated leftovers or anything you wanted to add to make a big pot meal. We ate chicken surprise with thin cornbread fried on top of the stove, or baked in the oven. With a little butter, sugar, eggs and a few other ingredients we could easily put together a dessert. There was always flour, and baking powder. Some of our desserts are well known today like chess pie, egg pie, white potato pie, sweet potato pie, buttermilk pie, tea cakes, and plain sweet bread. A big pot of pinto beans with seasoning meat and cornbread was considered a meal with leftovers.

Boycotts reminded me of our forefathers and surviving slavery. Don't misunderstand me, I know boycotts are like a drop in the bucket compared to the pain of slavery. I am only talking about how slaves survived with limited food.

Slaves learned to take what whites didn't want from the garden or field to create a healthy eating survival plan. Many of these foods we now know as healthy; like turnip roots, potatoes, all forms of greens, corn as grits, cornmeal and corn flour. Slaves even took thrown away parts from a hog as a main food. Some of these parts are sold today like pig feet, ears, tails, neck bones, skins, souse and chitterlings.

During boycotts, Blacks families ate a lot of garden foods, pork, chicken, fish, grits, rice, oatmeal, hotcakes, sweet bread, all forms of dry beans and peas. Sounds good, doesn't it? Well, I can tell you it was. The best thing about it was that families shared. It's so much easier to cook a big pot of a two pound bag of pinto beans, than two pots of one pound bags of pinto beans. Two or three families would come together; cook and fellowship at the same time.

During the boycotts life was working for Black families; and it shocked the hell out of White families. Many White women couldn't cook a decent meal. Many eating places were having problems too, because they didn't have cooks and dishwashers. Some of the White families I knew were eating a lot of peanut butter and jelly sandwiches. Their laundry was pilling up, and their homes needed to be cleaned. We were winning this battle, and many whites were helping us to win. I understand why slaves came together at night to share, fellowship, and thank God. All of this was and still is a part of survival.

Doing less than the best, is a waste of the sacrifices and struggles of others. Although I was born, raised and educated in Mississippi; I've never had a problem functioning or fitting in outside of Mississippi. In spite of the pain, fear, doubt and hurt; growing up in Mississippi has made me a well-rounded outgoing motivated Black woman eager to give back and living her dream.

Mama's parents: Minnie Lee (Kitchen) and John "West" Ervin

Godparents

UNDER THE HILL SECRET

Chapter 3

Our neighborhood was referred to as "under the hill", and that it was. On top of the hill was downtown Jackson. Downtown was huge; it had the Capital Building, museums, public library, courthouse, city hall, Federal Building, large major stories, drug stores, and the "all white" Central High School. Central High School was larger than the three nearby colored schools put together. The "colored" schools were nearby on the edge of downtown. There was Smith Robinson Elementary (gds. 1-6), Brown

Junior High (gds. 7-8), and Rowan High School (gds. 9-12). I know you've heard the phrase; on the other side of the tracks. Well, we lived down the hill on the other side of the tracks.

Under the hill was a secret place for us. This was a place of hard working people that had a bond that no white man could break or destroy. We had our Black owned churches, mechanics neighborhood convenience store, taverns, taxi cab, barber shop, beauty shop, and many families with homes and cars. There was also the white owned Avery Body Plant were Dad and many of the men worked. Under the hill was a clean place to live with cut lawns, many flowers, and no trash. If someone was in need, the whole neighborhood would help. I remember a many times Mama would have a fish fry to raise money for neighbors rent, medical bills, or just from being laid off. No matter what struggles our neighbors faced most neighbors were there to help. A many days Mama cooked extra large batches of food so it could be taken to other families in need. We even had times when other people had to live with us. We didn't talk about things that went on at home. Dad said, "What goes on in this home stays in this home. You never know what life may hold for you". In other words, it could just happen to you.

People living under the hill faced many of the same battles that other colors faced. Many rent houses were overpriced, and in need of repair. Mothers that worked as maids had to work ten hours instead of six or eight hours. These long hours gave them less hours to take care of their own families. Work hours for the men were constantly being cut by the hours or even days. In hindsight, much of this was "control". Less time with the family and less money for the family caused the family unit to get weaker. That's what the white man though, but we had a secret under the hill. The more battles, struggles, and hardships this neighborhood faced, the stronger we got. We began to pray more, sing more, preach about the struggle more, share more, care more, and thank God more for having each other.

One battle under the hill was the rising water in the spring and fall. I always felt that Jackson could do something about this rising water, but they wouldn't. Like clockwork, once or twice every year or two we had to evacuate by boat. For the life of me I couldn't understand how water could rise so quickly, with us having a short period of time to get out.

Why did this water rise during the day and never during the night? As I discussed the flooding with my sisters, no one ever remembered waiting up to a flood. To me, somehow or another, water was being released into our neighborhood. During the big flood of 1961, water rose to the white areas of town. Then for some reason the city of Jackson started talking about redoing the dam at Pearl River and diverting the water to what would later be Ross Barnett Reservoir. I could only theorize that water was released under the hill to protect buildings on top of the hill; and homes and businesses around Pearl River. It was hard to prove my point, but I did find some very interesting information. As an adult I started researching, and two articles gave me some clarity. The possible construction of the reservoir had been discussed and committees formed as early as 1957 (Sorrels; 1962). Would you believe it was completed in 1963? The latest information was found on The Angling Channel; FLW Mississippi Division @Ross Barnett Reservoir, MS in a March 18, 2017 release which stated:

"Flooding of the Jackson section of the Pearl River had been studied by the U.S. Army Corps of Engineers since 1930 and city leaders envisioned commercial and industrial benefits from land reclamation associated with flood control. The Jackson Chamber of Commerce prior to the completion of the reservoir promoted riparian land reclamation with industrial development, a new bypass for U.S. Highway 49 constructed upon a levee, straightening the Pearl River channel and potential navigation. Construction on the lake was completed in 1963, and the water level reached average capacity in 1965."

I needed clarity because as a child the rising water was a life battle for me. As the water would rise, the Red Cross would send out rescue boats to evacuate the people. When the water was too deep, a 3ft. wide plank was extended from the boat to the porch of the houses. Rescue workers would stand on both sides of the plank to hold people hands to assist them walking the plank into the boat. We called it, "walking the plank". The rescue workers would carry small children, sick or the elderly into the boat.

The last time we lived through a flood Mama got so upset that she told Dad, "Albert we are going to move from under the hill. I refuse to walk another plank, or be carried out by boat. These girls don't need to go through this Albert. I spend my time worrying about you and water moccasin snakes. Albert we need to talk about this!". Dad knew Lela Mae was upset; so all he could say was, "We'll talk, we'll talk".

Whenever it flooded Uncle Waddell would pick us up on top of the hill by Sears and Roebuck store. Mama would be mad, but us girls knew we were going to have fun with our cousins. They had six kids; two girls and four boys. There was Nadine, Linda, Dub, David, Grey and Mangle. There we were with four girls and my mom; along with them in a three bedroom house. Through love and unity they made it work. Dad always stayed home to move furniture about and help keep some of the water out.

When the water receded we went home. That last time was different. People living in rent houses on Mississippi Street had to move out on short notice. I didn't want to move from Mississippi Street. This was the most fun street under the hill. I could sit on our porch and look at the lights as the whites enjoyed the first half of the State Fair; anticipating our turn the second half. I didn't want to move because I loved this house, and it was next door to my godmother. It had a screened in front porch, and a big storage room off the back porch. The fence was lined with honeysuckle vines that filled the house with the sweetest fragrance when we opened the windows. There was a row of garages along the back yard. One garage was like a play house, another one Dad kept his garden tools and lawn mower in, and the other one he converted into a chicken coop. This property was being sold so we had to move.

Dad found a house the next street over, almost behind my godmother's house. There was a wide wooded area with a path to the next street. Mom and Dad made it clear that they didn't want me to go through the path without them knowing. I don't know why, but I started slipping through the path to visit my godmother. I didn't know I was putting my life in danger.

One day after slipping through the path, about twenty horses escaped from the stockades at the fairgrounds and started galloping through the wide track of land. As I was beginning to walk through the path I heard the ground shaking. People were shouting, screaming, horns blowing. Through all that noise I could hear my mother calling my name, "Minnie, Minnie where are you"? Then other people called my name too. It felt like everything was going in slow motion. As I ran through the path as fast as I could, the pounding noise got closer and closer to me. As I ran through the path I could see Mom standing with the back door open. By the time I made it to Mom and looked back, I couldn't believe my eyes. Horses were rushing through the woods and even the edge of the back yard. I was speechless. I was so scared that I felt my meat shook on my bones. I held onto Mom tighter than see held onto me.

I learned a great lesson that day. Mom and Dad knew I had learned a great lesson too. They didn't punish me, but my body punished me instead. I had an upset stomach and shakes for days. My parents never had to worry about me and that path ever again.

Our happy neighborhood with it secret started to change as people started to sale their homes and move out. Landlords stop doing any repairs to rent houses, almost like they wanted people to move out. To Dad's surprise there was a small leak in our roof over Bobbie Ann's and Barbara Nell's bed. The landlord didn't try to do anything to fix it. After Dad checked the roof out, he explained to the landlord about the condition of the roof; and the landlord didn't get it fixed or do anything. Mom made it clear that if he can't fix the roof, we shouldn't pay rent.

Mom had already started looking for a house near Aunt Fenen and Uncle Waddell. She was definitely on a mission. Two weeks later it started to rain again. This time it rained so hard that it started to leak in the kitchen, then the hallway. All night we could hear Mom and Dad go through the house checking for leaks.

The last straw came the next morning when the ceiling over Bobbie Ann's and Barbara Nell's bed collapsed as water poured out onto the bed. Dad got a galvanized tub and put it in the middle of the bed. You can imagine what the call to the landlord was like that morning. Dad repaired the roof as best he could; the landlord did nothing.

Mom was so upset that she took the rent money and used it as the deposit on another house. Our new house was about ten miles away in Cottage Grove Subdivision; often called Virden Addition. Within a few weeks we were moving out; and I felt like I was living the movie, "A Raisin In The Sun".

Minnie Pearl, friend and Albertine Bobbie Ann,
two friends and Minnie Pearl

THE COTTAGE GROVE EXPERIENCE

Chapter 4

Family home in Cottage Grove

Our new house had some things that I really loved. We had a large living room that opened into a formal dining room. We also had an eat-in kitchen with lots of cabinets. The bathroom had two doors, one leading to each bedroom. We even had hardwood floors. The yard, house and neighborhood were perfect. Our new school was only five minutes away. Behind the school were railroad tracks. This time on the other side of the tracks was Grove Park Golf Course; the first and only Black golf course in Jackson. Once again Mom, with Dad's help, had turned an ongoing impossible battle to win into a true blessing for our family. As Dad prayed for us and our new home, he also prayed for the hard heart of our old landlord.

We found out later, our landlord wanted us to move out in order to sale the land for a development around the Mississippi Coliseum and fairgrounds. He couldn't force us to leave, because Dad always paid on time or early. Dad had also improved the property with minor repairs and paint, not to mention the beautiful flowers and lawn. I bet he got more money for this house because we kept it so nice. Our old landlord really owed us money for overcharging us and neglecting his property. Our new house was only $10 more a month; larger, newer and we deserved it. Truly blessed we were.

For some reason I had a sad happy feeling inside. I was sad because my old neighborhood was being torn apart family by family, and street by street. Because of eminent domain, Black home owners were forced to sale. Even churches and businesses were forced to sale too. All the White land owners were happy to sale. Some Black landowners gave them pure hell by holding out to the very end. My godmother was holding out for more money and on principle. Her land was a large tract of land that also had an old Indian trading store that once belonged to her father. My godmother was one of the last people to sale and move.

After being forced to move; with much prayer, singing and crying our church stayed together. The under the hill people had won a great battle. The members stayed together under the leadership of Pastor S. L. Spann Sr., and a new brick church was built. My dad's name, Albert Smith, is on the cornerstone as a deacon. This church is a part of our family history; to be able to see the name Albert Smith carved into the cornerstone is memorable.

With money from selling our old church, money we saved, and donations from members and others a new church was built. On Sunday July 14, 1963 members traveled from the old church on Mississippi Street, to the new church at 2545 Newport Street. We had a police escort with people in cars, and those that wanted to walk; walked with the children. When the carpool arrived at church people were already there. So many faces I didn't know, but they were praising God with us. I had never seen anything like this that was so positive; and good for our people and this neighborhood. This church was special to the under hill people, and now to the people already in the neighborhood.

There was a short ceremony for the ribbon cutting, of which Pastor S.L. Spann Sr. did the honors. Then people started lining up to go in. There were the ministers, deacons, mothers, guest, choir and the rest of us. As I walked up the tall stairs, I felt like I was walking into a cross. Walking through the sanctuary doors was a long center isle with pews on both sides. The pews ended in a large open space with about six rows of pews on the right and the left of the open space. Pass the open space was the pulpit, then behind the pulpit was the choir stand, and at the very top the baptismal pool. Like I said, it was shaped like a cross inside. We were the first Black church that I knew of with an elevator. God has a way of blessing his people in the midst of a battle. Fairview was blessed with a larger, better church on dry grounds. Because of this blessing, the members decided to rename the church Greater Fairview Mississippi Baptist Church.

Many of the same people under the hill that attended Fairview were still attending. Many people from the neighborhood became members too. Many under the hill people went as far as to move in surrounding neighborhoods near the church. Pastor Spann and his family moved down the street from the church, and my godmother moved on the street right behind the church. I didn't live near the church, but I could still walk to church. I learned that the secret of under the hill had very little to do with the place itself, it was the love and unity of the people.

After moving to Cottage Grove, I wanted to do everything. I didn't know a school could have so many things for you to do. I enjoyed art, dancing and I really wanted to play the drums. I liked studying and looking at nature, but I loved the beat of those drums. Mom and Dad were so afraid that I was going to get stuck playing the bass drum like another girl in the band that they said no. Really I think they thought I wouldn't learn how to play those drums. Or, did they think drums were for boys? I came up with another idea; to run track. Mom said," Well" as Dad added, "You don't have much weight to run off. You are my little skinny Minnie". I begged, "Please let me try to make the team, please". I practiced so hard. I worked out seven days a week, sometimes twice a day. Being skinny worked in my favor; I made the team and was assigned to the hurdles, broad jump, high jump, and relay as needed. By 10th grade my coach gave me an old hurdle to practice with in my back yard. Boy did I practice. I can't say that I was a super track star, but I did qualify four years in a row for the state track meet at the end of the season. I ran track and was a book worm too. My parents didn't like the track uniform because it was too revealing, but they were proud of me and what I had accomplished.

On the other hand, Barbara Nell's mean streak turned into school and school activities. She played the clarinet in the orchestra, was a majorette in the marching bank and a member of the journalism club. During Barbara Nell's senior year she was voted a member of Miss Brinkley's court.

Barbara Nell in the Journalism Club (Standing row-2nd from the left)

Cottage Grove was good for our family. This was a neighborhood that was still building homes on vacant lots. Within three years of living in Cottage Grove, we were able to move from our rent house to buy one of the new homes that were being built. Dad put five hundred dollars down on the house. As our new home was being built, we were there every day checking it out. I was so proud of our house and bathroom. I had never seen a blue bath tub or blue toilet. Mama was in love with the washer being in the kitchen instead of a storage room off the back porch. Things just kept getting better. Bobbie Ann was married, and lived less than a block away. Aunt Fenen lived one street over; I could see my niece Marnetta and my cousins every day, even several times a day

Our new home was light yellow with a partial tan brick front. The yard was large, with two fig trees and one walnut tree in the back yard. Dad started planting all kinds of different roses. I loved cleaning this home. I cleaned the picture window and swept the front porch every Saturday. I cleaned that window so much, that one boy from the neighborhood came by every Saturday and said, "Miss Minnie you need to rest yourself". We would smile and laugh as I continued to work. My family use to tease me because they knew he liked me. The joke was, we didn't know his name so we called him, "Rest Yourself". This was and still is a happy house. Our happy house is missing Mom and Dad, but we will continue to fill it with family, friends, fellowship, love and fun. After fifty three years, The Smith Home is still the place to be.

When Barbara Nell was arrested and put in a stockade after marching in the spring of 1963, she vowed to leave Mississippi after graduation. So Barbara Nell enlisted in the U.S. Army. Soon after graduation the U.S. Army picked Barbara Nell up at home. The family was so sad that she was leaving, but understood why she enlisted. Barbara Nell was taken to Robert E. Lee Hotel, where she was shocked to find out that she couldn't enter the front door with the other enlisted whites. She had to go to the back to enter the service door. All Barbara Nell could think of was to get equal rights, and respect. Barbara Nell's power play to join the U.S. Army became another battle of her life.

The new Barbara Nell

As she walked through the service door, there was a large kitchen to the left. She could hear the normal sounds of a restaurant kitchen, along with the aroma of what was almost unbelievable to breathe in. Just to think that she will have a chance to meet and eat with the other enlisted ladies.

Once inside Barbara Nell was taken to an area where there were colored men. As her eyes moved through the crowd, she instantly realized that she was the only colored female in the group. The men were assigned rooms in groups, and Barbara Nell was assigned a room by herself. Shortly afterward a tray of food was brought to her room. The tray was placed on the desk, as she was told to put the tray outside her door when finished. Barbara Nell stared at the tray for about a minute. On the tray were fries, a hamburger, a plain cube of cake, and a carton of milk. Later Barbara Nell placed the partly eaten tray of food outside the door; as she felt that this meal was a big letdown. Barbara Nell's mind had already picked out the foods from the kitchen. As she lay across the bed she imaged herself eating fried chicken, turnip greens, fried corn, and other foods just like what she knew had been cooked. She fell asleep thinking things are going to get better. Things have to get better.

That morning as they were ready to board the bus, the Sergeant gave a pep talk, and proceeded to board them on the bus. It was a full bus so they boarded from the back to the front. The Sergeant pointed to some colored men to board, and then he continued to point as he filled the bus. There Barbara Nell was, on a segregated bus with no colored or white signs. Many people were talking about different things, but the conversation got loud as the whites talked about the dining room and nice hotel rooms. Why was the food served family style with them eating all they wanted? They talked about fried chicken, turnip greens, candied yams, fried corn, cornbread muffins, and ice tea. As Barbara Nell heard this she asked Leroy next to her what he had for dinner. Why did Leroy say, "A hamburger, fries, milk, and dry cake".

When the bus arrived at Anniston Army Depot in Alabama, the group unboarded the bus to enter a large hall. As Barbara Nell walked into the hall; the commanding officer starting shouting at her about her two inch heels damaging his floor. Barbara Nell quickly took of her shoes, and continued to walk. The commander continued to shout at her, "You dummy, you're walking on my floor and leaving prints". Looking down at her stocking feet, and behind her were three clearly defined footprints. Barbara Nell couldn't move, she didn't know what to do. A white girl rushed over to Barbara Nell and handed her a pair of footies. This was the first time Barbara Nell had ever heard the word "footies". What was she to do with them? The white girl said, "Put them on, put them on". She managed to put the footies on, and continued to walk to the designated area. Basic training was hard, but it was hard on everybody. Something Barbara Nell kept engraved in her brain was the value of her uniform. Her uniform made here equal to all U. S. citizens. She was to wear it proudly, respectfully, and it will cause others to respect her for her service.

Barbara Nell's biggest battle happened on her return trip home after basic training. As Barbara Nell entered the small town segregated bus station, she noticed a partial glass wall. This glass wall was separating the colored from the whites. The colored side was packed, but there were plenty of seats on the white side of the partial glass wall. Barbara Nell walked pass the partial glass wall, took a seat, and took out her book to read. People on the other side of the partial glass wall just stared at this young colored army woman brave enough to sit in the white section.

After some time three white boys entered the bus station. As Barbara Nell was reading these white boys took her book and tossed it back and forth between them. Then one of them threw the book on the floor. Then one of them threw a dime on the floor and said, "Nigger you know what to do, lay down and spread your legs", Barbara Nell didn't move or say anything. Instead of helping Barbara Nell, the people looked on through the partial glass wall. Out of nowhere a priest walked over and asked the boys to leave. The priest picked up her book and handed it back to her as she tried to say thank you. Barbara Nell was so scared that she was truly speechless. As her bus was announced; the priest started walking Barbara Nell to the bus. After getting a few deep breaths, she turned to thank the priest. But he was nowhere in sight. Barbara Nell asked the bus driver, "Where did the priest go"? The driver said, "There was no one with you. I didn't see a priest". Barbara Nell knew she wasn't crazy. She knew, and felt what had happened to her. She even heard some of the people on the bus quietly talking about how scared they were for her.

Barbara Nell had mixed feeling as the bus passed the Welcome To Mississippi sign. Her new home was the army, but her true home was

Jackson, Mississippi. Just seeing the family, having Mama's great cooking, and being able to tell Mom and Dad thank you, made the last few hours of great anticipation.

Albertine surprised Barbara Nell by picking her up at the bus station. Not only had Albertine learned to drive, she had her own little brown corvette convertible with tan interior. When Barbara Nell made it home, we had a great celebration of family, hugs, kisses, tears and food. Dad could now listen to Barbara Nell's army stories instead of telling his own.

Barbara Nell tearfully told her story about waiting to board the bus to come home. She told how three white boys took her book, tossed it back and forth between them. She told how one of them threw her book on the floor. And how another one threw a dime on the floor and said, "Nigger you know what to do, lay down and spread your legs". Also, how a priest showed up and asked the boys to leave. The priest picked up the book and gave it back to her. More importantly, he stayed with her as she started to board the bus. "Dad", said Barbara Nell, "The bus driver said he didn't see a priest walking behind me. I knew it happened because people were talking about it on the bus". Dad looked at Barbara Nell, then around at the other sitting in the living room. "Barbara Nell", Dad said, "The priest was you angle". Silence filled the room, nothing else needed to be said.

As we fellowshipped with family and friends, there was great tasting food and good conversation. Barbara Nell's boot camp stories were sad and funny. I really think Barbara Nell found a place and a way to express herself. She didn't have equality as she wanted it, but she did see great improvements. Dad was right when he said, "Doing your best really pays off", and Barbara Nell's new life proved it.

In the midst of all the conversations and laughter, Barbara Nell asked, "Albertine when did you learn to drive?" All Albertine could do was laugh. This gave me a chance to add tear dropping laughter. I even had to stand to tell this one. I started by setting the scene, and talking about our neighborhood worm hold digger. I said, "Everybody needs to give Albertine a hand, because it's a wonder she didn't knock herself out or have whiplash". "Barbara Nell", I said, "Do you remember the neighborhood field for playing ball, riding bikes, and just kid fun?" "Yes," she said. Then I started to tell my story.

Well Mr. John would dig worm holes all over the field. Kids use to tease him about his worm holes. So, Mr. John fixed the neighborhood kids by digging bigger and deeper holes all over the field. Then Albertine bought a car, but she couldn't drive it; so she decided to learn how to drive in the field. She had three people teaching her the basic of driving a stick shift. Albertine was driving in and out of holes. Some holes were so big that the whole car would go down in the hole and pop up out the other side. Albertine learning to drive was so funny that kids preferred to watch Albertine learn to drive than play ball. People would come outside to watch and laugh at Albertine learning to drive in and out of holes. Kids would be running all over the field from the car and Albertine. If the holes didn't stop Albertine the clutch would. One day I laughed so hard that I peed on myself.

Albertine having a car was great for our little group. We would pull up besides walking teens and say," Want to drag"? Then we would speed off. Teens would pay to rid in Albertine's car. During this time a quarter would do, because fifty cents would buy a gallon of gas. Teens helped us keep gas in the tank, because they wanted to ride in a convertible. People use to say that those Smith girls are independent girls that don't need boys. They were right, that's how our Dad taught us; and it was working.

Barbara Nell's new life exposed her to so many things. Why did Barbara Nell talk about growing up under the hill more than any other life experiences? To this day she still lives by our under the hill secret of love, sharing, caring, and unity. As I think of it, we all live under this principle. All four of us take part in helping cloth and feed the needy and shut-in. Albertine has opened her home a many times to young adults and sick relatives in need. Bobbie Ann partnered with a major hotel to use their used bath cloths, hand towels, towels, and bed linen to make care packages for the sick and shut-ins. She would go as far as to add baked goods. She made bibs, lap scarves and treat bags for nursing homes. Albertine and Bobbie Ann are known for working with Greater Fairview Church for passing out clothes, furnishings and food to the needy. I've worked with Rockford Rescue Mission for over fourteen years. I've tutored kids for over forty years, and never charged a parent one dollar. I freely give my time, service and resources to the needy. Barbara Nell has been honored in Le Vern, CA for her foster care home. She and her husband, Kent, have fostered twenty eight kids. Most of Barbara Nell's foster kids stay two to three years; are more. Some were even special needs. In all nineteen have graduated from high school. Over half went on to attend college, trade school or a training program. At the age of 72 Barbara Nell is still fostering a family of three that she has had for twelve years. Two has graduated from high school, and one is still in high school. Barbara Nell is a widow now, but must finish the task her and Kent started many years ago.

Our under the hill secret was really the biblical principle for life. With us, we didn't just talk about it, we lived it. I guess it isn't a secret anymore. Good secrets are meant to be shared.

REMEMBERING DAD

Chapter 5

My father, Albert Smith, was a very handsome man. Dad was six feet tall with broad shoulders, light medium brown wavy hair with light brownish gray eyes. Dad was determined to bring his family up in a Christian home. It seemed like Dad was always praying for our family day and night. A many nights I fell asleep hearing Dad praying in the next room, only to wait up the next morning still hearing his pray. As a child I thought he prayed all night. Now as an adult, I know he did go to bed, he only slept fewer hours than I did.

Dad wasn't an educated man, but he had a brilliant mind. Dad had a 3rd grade education, but knew and understood how to do algebra. A matter of fact he was the one that helped us with math. He said that algebra was like a guessing game with something missing. Math in our home was a "what if" game.

Dad taught us girls that it was best to work hard at everything we did. We were also taught that it was best to have our own money. To bring the lesson close to home; a story about his eighteen year old sister's death was told.

Dad had two living sisters, his twin sister Alberta, and his oldest sister Lula Ann. I grew up knowing my Aunt Alberta; she was a beautiful tiny version of my Dad with a sweet spirit about herself. Dad truly loved Aunt Alberta; I think it was because there were only two of them left.

Dad said that during the late 1020's, light skinned girls with long hair were attractive to colored and white men alike. His sister was also blessed, or as he put it, cursed with a small waist and big hips. Her beauty caused my grandmother, Mama Lula, to worry about her. She was worried because men whistled at her and made comments about her being high yellow and stuck up. Lula Ann was like any typical young person, she just wanted to be where the fun was. There was fun at the county fair. During that time there were two fairs; or as they called them, "Colored Fair" and "White Fair". The "Colored Fair" had men playing the guitar with singing and dancing. It had stage shows, games, people from all around and all kinds of soul foods, with pork chop sandwiches being the most popular food. Lula Ann wasn't dating anyone, so she went to the fair along just as she did the night before.

When it started getting late, Mama Lula started pacing the floor. Dad said she had a sad worried look on her face, almost as if she knew something had happened. She looked outside, walked outside and just wouldn't stop looking for Lula Ann. Mama Lula told the twins that they had to go look for Lula Ann because something was wrong. Before they could get out of the house people had ran to their house crying and screaming that Lula Ann was hurt. Mama Lula started walking and partly running in the direction of the fair. The crowd followed along. As mama Lula sped up, the twins did the same. When the crowd made it to the fair, there she was bleeding and all limp. She was dead! Dad said that Mama Lula just held her and cried, she rocked her like a baby. She screamed out, "Why, why?" People tried to tell Mama Lula what had happened, but Dad didn't think she heard them. He felt that Mama Lula was in shock because what she feared had happened. Her first living child out of eleven had not only been hurt, but had been killed.

It was strange that people could say what had happened, but no one could tell Mama Lula who killed her child. All the stories ended up being about the same. They said that Lula Ann didn't have much money, so she just walked around and socialized. Since so many people were buying pork chop sandwiches Lula Ann wanted one too. Several people offered to buy her a pork chop sandwich, but she refused to accept their offer. Finally, she agreed with this man to pay him back for the price of the sandwich. She had no idea that he meant she was to pay him back that night, and with her body. When this man angrily requested his money, Lula Ann asked him to give her time to get it. He tried to force himself on Lula Ann; after a struggle Lula Ann lay bleeding and the man was nowhere to be found. Dad said that people knew who this man was, but they didn't want to tell. The family also believed that Lula Ann knew this man, because she borrowed money from him, which was against Mama Lula's rule on borrowing. It was because of what happened to Lula Ann that Dad wanted us to always have our own money. We must never borrow from others, especially from men. As dad put it, "If you can't afford it, you don't need it".

When I was ten years old, Dad explained that we had to understand money if we didn't want people to cheat us out of our money, goods and land. Not understanding money has cost a many families much. He explained that it was more important to know how to do math in your head, rather than on paper. If someone is trying to cheat you on paper, you'll already know the answer because you are doing it in your head. People of all races will respect you when you can do this. People will think twice before trying to cheat you. They'll also spread the word about your skill.

To help us understand this concept better, Dad explained to us about how our grandfather and how he thought he died. Dad's family was share croppers, but they were constantly being cheated by the owner of the land. After years and years of being cheated, my grandfather decided to keep his own set of records. At harvest time my grandfather would do as always, only now he would do his math in his head. He also started correcting the land owner. At first the land owner would thank my grandfather for catching his mistakes, as time passed he started calling my grandfather a "smart red nigger".

My grandfather started keeping his own record book. He even did odd jobs to earn extra money. My grandmother started taking in washing and ironing. As time went on they had earned enough money to finish paying for the land, with a little money left over.

Trouble started when my grandfather went to pay off his land, and get his signed deed. The landowner said my grandfather owned more money. When my grandfather took out his own record book with dates, weights and amounts; the landowner became very upset. After much disagreement the landowner said my grandfather owned him over twenty more dollars. To the landowner's surprise my grandfather had $18 in bills, and a pocket filled with change. The total amount was counted out on the table as my grandfather demanded his signed deed. The landowner once again said he had misfigured the account, and he really owned his over thirty dollars. My grandfather couldn't take it anymore; so he picked up a whole ham from a nearby table and knocked him out. Granddad took back his money, and rushed home to let the family know what had happened. He gave most of the money to Mama Lula. Changing clothes and whatever food they had went into a flour sack. My grandfather left running through the woods and was never heard from or seen again. The word was that the klu Klux klans probably hanged him.

Dad was good with math, but he had trouble reading. Dad wanted to read better so he could read the bible to himself. Dad had such good memory that he could quote scriptures word for word. Miss Moose Anna was Dad's distant cousin and neighbor who agreed to help him read better. Some evenings we would walk up to Miss Moose Anna's house for his lessons. Miss Moose Anna's house was a fun house to visit, but it was scary too. Miss Moose Anna was a sort of settle lady that worked at the state fair when it came to town. She had this oversized mahogany piano that she couldn't play well, but she would guard it like gold. Later I found out that she kept bags of money behind this old piano. If I moved near this piano; or, oh my goodness touch it, she would give me that "look". She had those light brown piercing eyes. When she looked at me I felt like her eyes were talking to me. Believe me; I did exactly what her eyes said. If her eyes said, "don't walk near the piano"; I stopped and moved away. If her eyes said don't touch the piano; I wouldn't touch the piano. Those eyes even had a way of telling me to sit down. She was very clean, but her house smelled like mothballs. It made me feel like she was trying to cover up an odor. Miss Moose Anna had boarders coming and going; so maybe she though mothballs smelled good. Instead of watching me, she should have been watching her boarders.

A teenage boy named Sal Mineo came to stay with Miss Moose Anna for a time during the summer. Miss Moose Anna told my parents that she once worked for Sal's parents when she lived up north. She said Sal was always getting in trouble, and now he was hanging with a gang. Since Sal got along with her; the family sent him south until things cooled off. The people in our neighborhood found out that Sal could sing.

One day when we had a fish fry, Sal and a man called Cadillac Joe put on a show in our front yard. Cadillac Joe was playing his guitar, and Sal was singing and dancing. Other people were singing and dancing. My family and a few others were looking at the excitement through our screened in porch. All I could think of was grownups can sure act crazy at time. It was all in good fun.

Dad didn't want anybody to accuse him of seeing Miss Moose Anna, so it was decided by my parents that one of use girls would have to go with Dad at all times. We went there several times a week. When the weather was nice, and there was still plenty of sunlight; she would work with Dad on the front porch. When it was cold or dark they worked at a table in the living room only a few feet from the old mahogany piano. Dad's reading improved so well that Dad didn't need to go to her anymore. As years passed Dad was reading other things too, but he mostly read the bible.

I was afraid of Miss Moose Anna alive; I was more afraid of her dead. The way she died wasn't anything our neighborhood had ever experienced before. Miss Moose Anna's house caught fire and the blaze was seen for blocks. I had never seen a fire so big and so hot. The fire burned the house to the ground. Later I overheard my parents talking about somebody must have killed her, and set the house on fire. Her body was found unrecognizable curled up in a corner of the living room.

When Miss Moose Anna's family was notified, somebody notified Sal Mineo and he had a rubberlike cast of Miss Moose Anna's face, neck, and upper body made from a picture. I was told that it really looked like her. I really don't know because my parents wouldn't let me go to the funeral, because I was having nightmares. I wasn't really sleeping or eating; I was even seeing ghosts. My parents went to the funeral, and reassured me that this funeral was like any other funeral. They said that Miss Moose Anna looked like she was sleeping. Hearing that made me more afraid, how could this fake body look real? Did they put the burned up body in the bottom of the coffin? I just needed to get the image of the fire, her buried up body and the fake body out of my head.

Miss Moose Anna was a great teacher, Dad's reading improved quickly. He worked so hard at his reading; in the morning, on his lunch break, after work and before bed time. Dad's reading improved so well that he would help us pronounce the name of biblical characters. Dad became such a good reader that he was voted superintendent of the Sunday school. He held that position for over ten years. He also conducted laymen classes for the men of the church. Dad was really a good role model because he worked so hard at whatever he did.

Dad also told us to do the best at everything we did. First, because it was the right thing to do; and because, we would be wasting time and energy if we had to redo something that was half done the first time. To help us learn this lesson, we had to redo poorly done work. I remember having to redo cleaning the kitchen because I did a rush job. I rewashed the dishes, wiped down the counters and stove, swept and mopped the floor, and took out the garbage. I had to do the same thing each night for the rest of the week. I started cleaning the kitchen with a smile and a song. I did so well with the kitchen that my other sisters would trade dish washing nights with me, or pay me to do their dish washing night.

Dad had blood vessel problems in his legs that caused pain from time to time. One night Dad had leg cramps so bad that Mama shed a few tears herself. As Dad rubbed his legs with green alcohol, and repeatedly made attempts to walk; I could see how tight his calf muscles were. It looked like his legs had blood vessels that got larger and larger, and formed knots. I told Dad to stop trying to walk, that's when Dad told me that he had to walk on his legs or the muscles would lock. He looked at me and said, "Minnie Pearl you just have to walk it out, it'll get better honey. It's beginning to feel better already". Then I smelled the odor of coffee. Mama had put on a pot of coffee and was cutting Dad a slice of coconut cake. Within a few minutes Dad was sitting in his chair with his right leg stretched out as he rubbed on another coating of green alcohol. In walked Mama with a large slice of three layered coconut cake, and a cup of coffee with cream and sugar. Boy it smelled good, only if I could just have a sip of coffee. Maybe If I take the dishes to the kitchen, I'll have a chance to drink the coffee left in Dad's saucer. Mama gave us girls coconut cake too, only we had a glass of milk with our. As always we had to eat at the table. It didn't matter, just looking at Dad feel better made me feel all happy inside. My sad feeling was that I knew the pain wasn't gone forever, it was going to return. Nobody knew when the pain might return; tomorrow, next week, next month, but it would return.

As I overheard Mama and Dad talking, Dad was expressing his thankfulness for his pain. He said, "Sister the pain means I still have legs. I have legs that I can walk with, and take care of this family with. Yes Sister, thank God for the pain". To my surprise Mama didn't say anything, she just gave him this acceptance look with a one sided smile. As she got up to collect the dishes she gently placed one hand on Dad's shoulder and paused for a few seconds; then she went into the kitchen.

Dad had a way of telling us stories about respect and hard work. Some of those stories really made me think about life. One story was about sweet potatoes and peanuts. As he told us the story he said I was around four or five, and he was around forty seven years old. Dad said he was spending too many hours standing on his legs, so they started to swell very badly. He was going back and forth to the VA Hospital for treatment. The VA wanted to cut one leg off, and treat the other leg. Dad prayed about his legs and decided that he was going to die with two legs not one. Instead of working full time Dad started to work part time.

Mama and Dad had their little private meeting; and decided that they could make up the money that they would be missing by selling small sweet potatoes pies, and bags of roasted peanuts at the plant. The plan of action was to have the neighborhood sweet potato man to stop by twice a week. They would buy sugar and flour by the large ten pound sacks. They would buy several large bottles of flavor from the Raleigh Man each time he comes. Butter was easy to come by because so many people in the neighborhood got government commodities. Neighbors would be happy to barter butter for fresh garden vegetables. Lunch bags were super cheap in bundles of fifty or one hundred. All Dad had to do was pass the word the three days he worked, and they would be in business.

As always, Mama was organized. Dad said I even got into the picture; I was the sweet potato man caller. When I would hear the sweet potato man coming, I would run through the house repeating everything he said, "Sweet potato man, big nice sweet potatoes". When I finished running through the house, I would go and stand at the door as I repeated to say, "Sweet potato man" in a deepened voice. They said I kept this up until they stop selling sweet potato pie and peanuts.

Dad said that Mama would get up before day to start boiling her sweet potatoes, and roasting peanuts. Then she would start making pie crust, and fit them into little pie pans. When she finished the pie crusts, she would start cooking breakfast. While Mama fixed breakfast, Dad would bag the roasted peanuts and put them in a box on top of a hot water bottle. As soon as Dad and my sisters were out the house; Mama would start mixing pie filling, putting filling into the crust, and then into the stove. The stove would be filled with three racks of little pies. As soon as these were done, in went more pies. While the last set of pies was cooking, we would get dressed and fix Dad's lunch. As the last sets of pies were coming out of the stove, Mama would also put them in a box with wax paper between each layer of pies. When the last pies came out the oven, we would be off to Dad's job with my wagon filled with two boxes of pies and peanuts. We would always make it there before the lunch horn sounded. Dad would sell all the pies and peanuts in no time, and still have time to eat lunch. Mr. Avery, Dad's boss, even had Mama to bake pies for him; only he would come to the house to pick his pies up. By the time the horn sounded again, we would be on our way home. Only this time I would be riding in or pulling the wagon home.

When we made it home, we would have our lunch, and Mama would count the money. Mama would always write the total down. This would help Mama and Dad keep up with their profit. Dad said we almost made as much money selling pies and peanuts a few days a week as he did working all week at the plant.

Dad was such a hard worker that he got a few yards to cut on Saturday. Then his yard business grew. In order to have our own money, Dad taught us to work, and save a portion of our earnings. By the time I was eight or nine I started to go with Dad to cut yards along with my sisters. Oh yes I know, we're girls and yard work is for boys. Dad taught us that "honest work" is fine if it doesn't hurt our bodies. Let's face it; yard work didn't hurt our bodies. Teasing from kids in the neighborhood about us cutting yards hurt our pride, but it hurt their pride more when they had to ask us for money or a share of our treats. Dad would pay us fifty cents from each yard. He taught us to save twenty five cents out of each dollar, and to put ten cents out of each dollar in church. That was sixty five cents out of each dollar to spend. Out of my three sisters, I saved the most. I would save fifty cents out of a dollar. Some weekends I would make two or three dollars. Two or three dollars was a lot of money in the late 1050's and early 1960's for a kid.

One of the funniest things to me was when the family of kids that teased us constantly about cutting yards; started cutting yards too. These kids teased us in school, in the neighborhood, and even at church. The joke really came when life turned the table on this family. Times had gotten bad, and most factories cut the work week down to three days a week. It was so funny to see this family do the same thing to make ends meet, "yard work". Dad had a new lawn mower, and they had an old one. We had a few large yards of well to do people, they had whatever they could get. Mama made us pants to wear, and the girls in the other family wore boy pants. We never pointed the finger, or made fun of them; we just looked at them with a look of "What goes around comes around". When I was along with my sisters, we would laugh and laugh. Afterwards the strangest thing of all happened; these kids stopped teasing us once they had to do the same to make ends meet.

Dad was a strong man inside and out. I saw my Dad cry four times. My Dad cried when his mother, his twin sister and my brother died; also when I was hurt in a lawn mower accident. Mama Lula lived a full life and she died in her late seventies. Dad's twin, Alberta, died in her late fifties which was a shock to everyone. During her illness we or Dad would go by train to visit her on some weekends. When Dad heard that his twin had passed he just started running as fast as he could. He was crying and running trying to make it to his sister. He returned over an hour later, and just cried like a baby. I remember his saying, "I should have been there for her, I should have been there". We cried with him. When my brother, Robert, died; Dad went into a daze and had to be taken to the VA Hospital for irregular heartbeats. When he finally accepted Robert's death, he just sat on the side of his bed and cried in silence. I don't think he hear the rest of us. He also cried when my three toes were sliced by a lawn mower.

One Saturday Dad was doing his lawn service work, when his lawn mower just quite. As he and another man worked on the mower, I decided to watch. I don't know whether I was standing too close, or this lawn mower decided to cut toes instead of grass. To our surprise the lawn mower started up, and within seconds had cut off my big toenail, and sliced two other toes. My toenail flew from under the mower and landed in Dad's hand. The lawn mower stopped, as blood just started to flow on the sidewalk. The homeowner got me towels, and rushed us to the hospital. My Mama met us at the hospital. Before surgery Dad was praying for my foot as tears ran down his face. When I woke up he was still praying as tears ran down his face. He felt responsible for what had happened; but I didn't think it was anyone's fault. Accidents do happen. I had to prove to Dad that I was just fine. Later that day I hopped next door to visit my godmother to share the experiences of my "battle scares". Indians seem to give the impression that you are a better person when you have overcome some difficulty in life.

I truly believed that Dad tried to be like the father he didn't know or have. He was a true provider and leader of our family. I do understand the statement, "Time brings about a greater understanding". As a child I didn't understand why Dad prayed so much; as an adult I understand that being thankful for a little can develop into much. Dad did grocery shopping on Fridays at Liberty Grocery Store after cashing his check. When he made it home we would have the table filled with bags and bags of groceries. Before we could touch a bag, we had to pray for the food we had received. We would have so much food that we almost didn't have a place to put all the food. Dad made comments like, "I couldn't pass up this good buy, and someone will eat it". I now know that he wasn't only talking about our family, he was also talking about anyone that may come to the house in need. Very early on Saturday morning we would walk to Colonial Day Old Store, called the Bread House. Dad would get five loaves of bread for a dollar. We would also get honey buns, and all kinds of snack cakes for little or nothing. We would eat some kind of snack on the way home as we listened to Dad tell us one of his interesting life stories.

Dad went out of his way to help others. I even remember when Dad gave a man a suit with the shirt and tie to match. Dad told Mama that he knew this man wasn't the greatest provider, or role model for his family, but the suit may be what he needed to go to church. The suit of clothes will remove one of the man's excuses for not going to church. Dad's generosity didn't make this man a churchgoer, but it did influence his family to attend more.

Dad did do family outings or just have quality time with us. Almost everywhere Dad went, other than work, one or two of us girls went with him. We were so proud of our Dad, he always tried to look nice and neat. Dad wore a hat almost everywhere he went. He was well groomed with a haircut every other week. Sometimes he would do his nails, or Mom would do them for him. He would polish his shoes at night, and taught us to do the same. One outing was going to the colored Alamo movie theater on Farish Street. I remember walking in twos holding hands: Bobbie Ann and Barbara Nell, Albertine and me, and bring up the rear was Mom and Dad. After the movie Mom and Dad would buy hot tamales on Farish Street to take home.

I finally met Dad's father when I was around ten or eleven years old. This bald headed light skinned old man carrying a briefcase came to our home when Dad was at work. Mom went to the screen door and said, "May I help you"? The old man said, "Is Albert Smith here"? Mom said, "No he is at the plant". Looking tired; he sat in a chair on the porch. Mama quickly sent one of us to get a glass of water. On returning with the water he quickly drank the full glass. He handed the glass back to Mama and said, "Thank you". As he started to talk he did a short version of what Dad said about his Dad leaving. As he was talking Mom introduced herself and us to the man. Then he said, "Do you have a coke"? Mom said, "No, but I can fix you a glass of ice tea or lemonade". "No thanks" he said; "Is there a store around here"? "Yes, up the street", Mom said. To make a long story short, he sent Albertine and me to Miss Elnora's store to get one coke; yes one coke. Albertine and I returned with his one coke. After opening the coke, he looked at us and offers us a swallow. We both shuck our heads no. He opened his briefcase and took out a BC; then he put the powder in his coke. I starred at the man; as I thought to myself he was too cheap to be Dad's Dad. Mama finally let him come inside as she went in and out of the kitchen finishing dinner. Us girls had to stay in the living room with the old man.

When Dad made it in from work, he walked in the door and stared at the man. They spoke to each other. Mama said, "Albert do you know who this is"? Dad slowly said, "No". Mama said, "Albert this is your dad". Dad said, "My dad is dead". He said, "No son they didn't catch me. I shaved my head, and started living deep in the country. I even acted like I couldn't read or write. I had to do what I could to live". He went on to say that he did write Mama Lula, but had to mail the letters from little towns around where he lived. He didn't put his address or real name on the letters because they would find him. Then he said, "How is your mother"? "She is died", Dad said. Dad continued, "Why now"? The man went on to tell Dad that he was sick, and needed to see his family. My Grandfather only stayed two days. As he left they hugged, and Dad said, "I'll see you next time Dad. Call me, you have my number now". We waved as the cab pulled off.

Dad provided for us and did everything he could to educate use. Dad provided for me when I went to college, as well as helped my cousin because of her families' financial problems. Aunt Lillian and Uncle T.C. couldn't afford to pay room and board at the college, so Tommie Cene moved in with us and shared my bedroom. It was similar to sharing a dorm room, only we had to share a bed too. It all worked out because after picking Tommie Cene up on Fridays, they would bring her back with food from the country. Dad didn't charge them anything, but it was like they were paying us with food. We were just family, caring for family. It was just great for me, because I had a good roommate that had some of the same interest as I did. I had a cousin that became my best friend. Dad didn't make a difference in use, he gave both of us money at the end of the week for the upcoming week. He would say, "I know it isn't much, but it'll last if you spend it wisely". Dad continued to do this for the full school term, until their financial problem was solved. Dad continued to motivate me, and have our father daughter talks. The world was changing, and he knew I needed to be ready to change with it. As we sat outside in the cool of the evening, Dad used nature to help me understand life in general. He was right; insects, plants, birds, worms and squirrels respond to changes in the weather. Surely I had to make changes to changes in my environment too. Dad's simple words and analogies were so true and memorable,

"I've never seen a squirrel act like a rabbit, and I've never seen a rabbit climb a tree. But, I've seen a squirrel collect food to store up for changes in the season. An ant can even have so much determination, that it can carry a crumb several times its size and weight. Minnie, in life you need to make changes to better yourself, but never change the true you. Never change your value system, or the beautiful Christian woman that you are. Just like that ant you can do great things. I believe in you, and your mother and I know you will not forget what we have put in you. Pray about the changes you face and make, and let God direct you. I have followed this advice from time to time for the last 48 years. Would you believe the following day after our talk I received a letter in the mail with my student teaching assignment. That letter shocked me in a way that it brought back memories of the civil rights movement. I've been assigned to Central High School in downtown Jackson, Mississippi. Why me? I didn't have this school on my list. Why did I have to be the first Black student teacher at Central High School? I didn't feel safe. HELP ME DEAR GOD- ANOTHER BATTLE!!!

Central High School had a reputation of being the high school where KKK kids attended. It was built like a fortress in 1888 (The Clarion Ledger.com Jackson, MS local; Central High School Jackson, MS; June, 1969), and it even had security. Jackson had received a final mandate to desegregate its schools. Many white parents took their kids out of public schools and put them in private schools. Some parents were so determined to retain the heritage of Central High School that they let their kids stay at Central High School. I didn't have one class to teach me about how to deal with hatred and prejudice attitudes. I knew I had to go into this situation prayed up, and with an open mind.

My first day at Central was really something. I had a chance to attend my first staff meeting. I was hoping to meet the other Black student teachers, but there was none. When I say none, I mean none. I was the only student teacher period; not another Black one, no White one, no other student teachers. The only other person I knew was my high school trigonometry teacher. I was the only girl in his trig class of ten, and I am now once again the only female in another strange situation. Mr. Henderson made me feel so good when he told me that he knew I was going to make it in life. He said, "Smith, you have the looks, class and most of all the knowledge to be a great teacher. Let me know if you need my help, I'll be here". Those words assured me, and gave me a support system.

My first day in the classroom was overwhelming, not in a really bad way. As students walked in the classroom door, I said "Good morning". Would you believe these 10th graders were hitting on me, they were even talking about my body. I am a "hot babe, stacked with big legs, and young". After the bell rang I was introduced to the class as the student teacher for the next ten weeks. By lunch time I had students coming by the room to see the new Black student teacher. I just smiled, and believe me I did have a great day.

The person that didn't like me was my principal. That was really ok; by the end of my student teaching he had learned how to respect me for my professionalism. I wore a lab coat each day. I wore heels when entering and leaving the building, and even in the lunch room. In the classroom I wore flat shoes.

Mrs. Robinson was my lead teacher, of which she was a great teacher. Mrs. Robinson's command of the class was superior. At times the white students would just start talking and turning their backs to Mrs. Robinson. Mrs. Robinson had to remind them that she was in control of their grades. Poor grades would follow them throughout high school interfering with sports and college. After her short talk; students listened, worked, and interacted with each other. True learning was taking place. Surprising to see was the level of friendship in the class. Most of the white boys and a few of the white girls stayed to themselves. The other sat and worked in assigned groups. A few friendships did form. The oddest friendship was between a small framed Black boy with a limp, and a White football player. They were friends in the classroom, but strangers outside the classroom door.

On one rainy day after school I had the opportunity of giving Fred a ride four blocks down Mill St. As I drove in the hard down pour, I asked about Fred's friendship with Lloyd. Fred simple said, "Lloyd needs me, and I need him. Lloyd needs to stay out of trouble and keep his grades up cause he wants a scholarship to Old Miss. Lloyd is my lab partner, and together we get 'A's" and "B's". The White kids tolerate Lloyd cause he is one of the star players for football and basketball. Students tolerate me cause they don't want to upset Lloyd. One lab day the White boys were acting up, and wouldn't listen to Mrs. Robinson. Lloyd stood up, and told the Whites to get in their seats and shut up. The room was silent. Mrs. Robinson thanked Lloyd and we finished the lab that day with an "A".

As we continued to talk, Fred felt that I am seeing a different class from the first months of school; "Miss Smith, these kids didn't want us here, some still don't. The rich ones went to private schools, and the poor ones had to stay. I am here cause I can walk to school, and 'cause I hate riding a school bus. I just want to do my work, and graduate. We just need more Black teachers. We need teacher like you, teachers that care.

As I pulled over to let Fred out; he said, "Thanks Miss Smith". I smiled and said, "You are welcome". He said, "Thanks for being you; you and Lloyd have helped me to make it through this year. Thanks for the ride and talk." As I pulled off; he waved, and I said, "See you tomorrow".

As I was doing my student teaching I was also taking Physics II. Dr. Curry excused me from class for the term with the understanding that I would turn in all assigned work along with labs, and I must pass the final. Dr. Curry even decided to temp me a little; he said, "If you turn in all assigned work, I will give you the grade you make on your final exam". You know I took that offer. I worked my butt off. I just loved working under pressure. I worked so hard that by April 10th I had read all assigned readings, and turned in all assigned work. By April 24th I had completed my student teaching, and had returned to my Physics class. I got back into my study group, as if, I had never left. I was ready for my final exam. This exam was very long, but I knew the work. Not only did I finish it early, I went back and double checked it. I gladly turned it in with a smile. The only part I worried about was a lab he added to class that wasn't on the syllabus. When Dr. Curry handed me back my exam booklet on Monday, I wanted to hug him; but you know I didn't. Written on my exam booklet was "93.5%"=B+". I am all good; I had an <u>A</u> for student teaching, and a <u>B</u> for Physics.

Now that my student teaching was over I still didn't understand my student teaching assignment. I didn't even understand why the few Black teachers at Central would chose to teach there. I really didn't think they wanted to teach at Central. I definitely can't understand why Mr. Henderson would leave modern Brinkley High to come to old Central High. Maybe he and the other teachers were placed her not by chose. Hopefully one day the truth will all come out. On November 15, 2017 a "gold nugget" fell in my hand. While browsing the Jackson Free Press I came across a very enlighten article by Arielle Dreher; titled, "How Integration Failed in Jackson's Public School from 1969 to 2017". Dreher included information about Central High School during the same school year I did my student teaching at Central High School. The article talked about Brenda Walker a student that attended the school year of 1969-1970, I don't want to lose any of the meaning or emotions Brenda felt so I would like to share it with you just as Dreher wrote it.

"It was a cold winter day in 1969, but Brenda Walker was not thinking about the weather when she put her coat in her locker. After all, Central High School in the middle of downtown Jackson had radiators to heat the classrooms.

Central was traditionally an all-white-high school, but Walker was one of a handful of black students who opted to attend Central despite little encouragement from family or friends. Black students were allowed to voluntarily integrate white schools in Jackson after Congress passed the 1964 Civil Rights Act.

When Walker walked into her biology class, she noticed all the students sitting on the side of the room nearest the door-but that was not unusual. She was usually the sole black student in her classes, and she was accustomed to her white counterparts never sitting in the same row as her due to her race. This day, however, she noticed that her classmates wore coats and hats. As she took her place in a row of her own next to the window, she realized the large pans were wide open. She had walked into a trap, and she was stuck.

"Oh God, they planned this," she thought to herself, realizing that she could not just get up to go to her locker for her coat and still get back to class on time.

The biology teacher, who Walker remembers was not white or black but cannot recall his name, came in and began teaching. Walker, the only black student in class, was shivering. The white students, bundled in their coats and hats, were warm and smug. The biology teacher walked over to the window and began closing them one-by-one as he taught. Soon, the class was stifling hot, and the white students began to remove their gear.

"No, everyone that has a coat or a hat on leave them on until the next period," the teacher told the class. Walker remembers that day with gratitude because her biology teacher at least in an indirect way acknowledged the discrimination she had experienced".

I had been put in the middle of a crucial time in Jackson's integration process. The Supreme Court was fed up with dozens of states doing their form of integration, which was really segregation. On October 29, 1969 the U.S. Supreme Court demanded an integration plan from Jackson immediately. The Supreme Court said, "Continued operation of racially segregated schools under the standard of 'all deliberate speed' is no longer constitutionally permissible. School districts must immediately terminate dual school systems based on race and operate only unitary school systems".

Now I know why I was caught up in the middle of this process. Central High School wasn't on my list of schools, but Jackson Public Schools was. I guess they only needed one of me; that's one Black student teacher. Still in the back of my mind there should have been another student teacher regardless of race assigned to Central High School. Well, I did have a student teaching assign near home, which saved me money. I was also near the college if I needed to use the Physics lab, or use resource materials.

To some it might seem like I am complaining a little. Really I am not complaining, I am answering questions that I've had for over forty five years. I've received answers to questions that were partly answered; now I have the complete answer or the rest of the story. I feel like that little girl finding a four leaf clover in a field of clovers.

May 1970 was to be the highlight of my life. But in the month of April things were moving so fast. On April 27th my Anatomy professor called me into his office for a conference about my future. Since I was in a dual track of education and premed, he needed to know which direction I had decided to go in. As we talked, I informed him that my family was poor and couldn't afford medical school. I expressed to him how much I enjoyed my student teaching experience, and how I truly wanted to teach. He looked at me and smiled as he opened a blue folder on his desk. "Smith," he said, "I need you to hear me out before you say anything". I said, "Yes Sir". He continued, "You have a quality that many school districts are looking for. Integration has opened a big door, Smith you are qualified and able to walk through that door". As I tried to speak he said, "Hear me out. You have the knowledge, motivation, experience and professionalism. Smith you even has the look and the voice. Smith you don't need to look for a job; jobs are looking for people like you. In this folder I have a job for you that will start you out with $2,000 more than if you stayed in Jackson to teach. Well what do you think?" I didn't know what to say, I just looked at him. "You can speak now," he said. He went on to say, "Let me tell you about the job. This job is in Waukegan, Illinois; about an hour outside of Chicago. This district is predominantly white, but is integrated. Remember this is the north. All I want you to do is go in for an interview. If you don't like what you hear walk away; if you like it let them see the Smith we know, your transcript will speak for itself. Recommendations are not a problem". I finally let out a few words, "Why me?" He went on to explain that this district had children whose parents were at Ft. Sheridan Navel Base. Waukegan was recruiting at traditional Black colleges and universities to get their best to help their school district comply with federal guidelines, and remain the best. "Listen Smith, I am sorry for the short notice, but the recruiter will be here on Monday. Will you be ready?" I took a deep breath and said, "Yes I will, thank you so much". He then gave me an informational packet from the blue folder. He looked directly in my eyes and said, "To save time I've included two unofficial transcripts, and two letters of recommendations from me. Make sure you keep a copy of each for your records. I need you to follow the check list to the letter. Smith we are counting on you. If you walk through this door, it will remain open for others to walk through too".

I remained in the professor's office discussing the packet and Illinois; a place I'd never been. I needed to talk to my parents before going forth with these plans. In the back of my mind I was also thinking of Lewis Stewart, my fiancé that had been drafted in March 1969. Moving to Illinois would work out, because Lewis was living in Rockford, Illinois before being drafted. We had planned to get married after he finished his military duty.

I also had a fear of the Vietnam War, and possibly becoming a widow. More import, I wanted to live on my own and manage my own finances before getting married. I had all these things on my mind, and things were moving too fast. Not to mention, I had to get ready for graduation and my family gathering afterward.

The interview went well. I was interviewed by Mr. Geir, the principal of Thomas Jefferson Junior High School. I followed the checklist to the letter. I also had the exit evaluation form Mrs. Robinson of Central High School. I left that interview with a smile. The following week I received an offer letter for a science position at Thomas Jefferson Junior High, and an application form. I did accept that position with a smile and a prayer.

Remember I said that May 1970 was to be the highlight of my life? There I was with a summer job, a teaching position for the fall, and many colleges protesting the Vietnam War. Looked like all hell was breaking loose; Jackson State had a small group of students protesting and demonstrating on campus. One problem was a public street that went straight through the campus that connected the west side of Jackson to the downtown area. Of all the possible street names; this street was named Lynch Street. Historically, white motorists would drive down Lynch Street intimidating and harassing campus students. This had been happening the four years I was at Jackson State, but I had only seen it with my own eyes twice. By not living on campus I didn't see what was going on at night and weekends, I only heard about it from other students. Things were getting so bad that many students were staying in their dormitories, going out only when they had to.

My cousin, Tommie Cene was staying close to her dorm room. With about two weeks left in the term, Tommie Cene just wanted to take her final exams and go home for the summer. Tension was building as campus students were protesting; as white Lynch Street motorist continued to intimidate and harass campus students. Hearing the news on May 4th that four students had been killed protesting at Kent State University in Ohio added fuel to the protest. What made these killings more tragic was that the Ohio National Guards had open fire on the protestors. It was reported that twenty eight guardsmen fired between sixty one to sixty seven shots in only thirteen seconds toward a crowd of protestors in a parking lot.

Four students were killed and nine were wounded (Kent State University Libraries; May 1-4, 1970).

Groups continued to form and protest throughout the campus. On May 14th a small riot broke out after hearing the news that in Fayette, Mississippi Major Charles Evers (brother of slain Jackson, Mississippi Civil Rights activist Medgar Evers), and his wife had been killed. Lynch Street motorist complained to the Jackson Police Department about campus students throwing rocks at them as they traveled Lynch Street. Seventy five armed city policemen, and Mississippi State Police responded to the call. On May 15th after a confrontation at 12:05 am in front of the library; shot were fired for thirty seconds at the students, the female dorm Alexander Hall, and the surrounding areas. As shot were fired, students scattered screaming, crying, moaning as they tried to get indoors and even drag other students inside too. (Jackson State University; May, 1970)

When gunfire ceased, two were left dead and twelve injured; of which one was sitting in the dormitory lobby. Phillip Lafayette Gibbs a twenty one year old pre-med student lay dead with two double buck shots to the head, a third pellet beneath his left eye, and a fourth under his left armpit. James Earl Green, a seventeen year old senior at Jim Hill High School was killed walking home from work at a nearby grocery store. As Green stopped to watch he was struck in the right side of the chest. The FBI investigator reported that over four hundred and sixty rounds struck Alexander Hall, shattering all of the windows facing the street on every floor. There were one hundred and sixty bullet holes in the outer walls of the stairwell. (Jackson State University; May, 1970)

The police and state troopers left the campus soon after the shooting, once they had picked up their shell casings. The National Guardsmen replaced the police and state troopers, then the ambulances were called in. (Jackson State University; May, 1970)

Tommie Cene endured the shooting, glass breaking, screaming and crying by hiding under her bed. Tommie Cene was so afraid that she didn't know when to come from hiding, or how long she had been hiding. When she did come out she could barely walk because her knees were numb. Our family was so thankful that she was safe.

I was left hurting for the families of the deceased, the wounded, and those that were scared for life. I was also left hurting because graduation had been cancelled. I will not walk across the stage to receive my degree. Did I cry? Yes I did. Once again this is a life battle. No one is a winner in this battle, no one.

I was so hurt and stressed out that I needed to spend more time with Dad. It was time for one of our little father daughter talks. I needed to make sense of it all. Our best talks were outdoors as we enjoyed nature. As always he knew the right thing s to say, and how to say them. I only pray that I will be able to share on this level with my children one day. Words of wisdom are worth more than money.

After graduating from Jackson State College, I did accept the teaching job in Waukegan, Illinois. To make sure I was well taken care of, Dad took me to Deposit Guaranty National Bank to take out a loan for $500, 00. I also had saved money from my summer job. Dad wanted to make sure I had enough money until my first paycheck. This money had to be used for my airfare, rent deposit, first month rent, transportation, and meals. With the money I had saved and money from Dad, I had more than enough money for two months. With all the skills Dad taught me about the value of money, I did just as I was taught. I only spent money when I needed to. I believe that I could manage my money well because Dad told me that he knew I could. By Dad believing in me, I had to live up to his expectations.

As always, Mom and Dad prayed for me constantly. I could feel a protective presence constantly around me. As I left for the airport, I got hugs from my family and friends. Dad gave me a little talk that ended with," I know you will do well. Minnie Pearl don't forget what we've taught you. Remember God in everything you do. No matter what happens, you can always come back home to us". As he cleared his throat, and looked into my eyes, he slowly said, "you are a lady now. We love you". Then he gave me a strong pausing hug. Dad was so motivated that he didn't know when to retire. Mr. Avery told Dad that it was best that he retired because of his leg problem. Dad was of age and had worked over thirty five years on the job. Dad still had his lawn service, only he was cutting for two families from when he first started his lawn service. I remember the Ward family very well. Mama called them the Ward sisters. They would invite Dad inside out of the sun to have lunch at the kitchen table. At first Dad didn't trust those three Ward sister, but they were just being good Christians. Dad was safe because two of us girls would be with him at all times. Eventually he was okay with it. Eventually the Ward sisters had Bobbie Ann, and Barbara Nell doing little work inside the house for then.

They had a habit of sending Mama something, and Mama had a habit of sending them something too. Mama would send things like baked goods, and they would send things like cloth napkins, scarves and lady like things. They finally became best friends. My mother never visited them at their home or called them, but they would call and come to the house and act like family. After one of their visits Mama said to Dad, "Do they realize that Cottage Grove is a Black neighborhood?" Dad didn't answer, we all just laughed. Later we found out that they didn't have friends, they kept to themselves. For some reason they just loved our family. As the Ward sister started to die out, and a brother moved in with them; the friendship continued. When all had died except one, she came by the house with a very large gold framed painting of Jesus. She wanted our family to have it because we loved Jesus. To this day the painting of Jesus remains in the living room on the wall behind the sofa.

Mr. Avery and Dad would talk from time to time. For some reason Dad still wanted to work at Avery Body Plant. By this time the plant had moved from under the hill to about a mile from the house. After a year of retirement, Mr. Avery offered Dad a night watchman job on weekends. Dad was so proud to still be working at 72. Dad used his work time as meditation and bible reading time. On Fridays Mama would send Dad a hot dinner around 7:00pm by Albertine when he would be doing a front gate check. Mom would usually send fried chicken, fish, or pork chops with all the works. One time when I was visiting from Illinois, I went with Albertine to take dinner to Dad. It reminded me of one of our father daughter talks. After an hour long visit, we left on the next front gate check. Although Dad had reoccurring leg problems, he continued to work weekends until he was seventy five.

I was most proud of my Dad a year later when he gave me away at my wedding. This was the first time Dad had ever wore a tuxedo. Here was my Dad giving me away as a young virtuous Christian woman, a true lady. As we walked down the aisle; I had to remind Dad to slow down. All in all, I wouldn't replace one thing on my wedding day relating to my Dad. He was perfect, and most of all he was my Dad.

Even with his age, Dad continued to touch the lives of many people, Black and White. I don't think Dad viewed himself as a senior citizen. He spent many hours a week at the Golden Key Nursing Home conducting their bible study group, and Sunday school lesson classes. He was constantly telling seniors to move their bodies and use their minds. He was right; these actions helped him to live a full productive life.

As our family grew the grandkids loved him. They enjoyed his stories just as much as we did. I was overjoyed to see them willing take in all the wisdom and knowledge he had to give. This kind of interaction is what keeps family history going from generation to generation. Just as I enjoyed walking and holding Dad's hand, the grandkids have taken on this same role. As I looked at their faces I felt the joy I once felt as I partly skipped holding Dad's hand as we walked.

For some reason Dad didn't age like many other senior citizens. I heard it said that Mama being twelve years younger, and us girls being born later in his life was keeping him young. I really don't know because Dad always did things with us, and now I see him doing the same with the grandkids. As I look at Dad on each visit; I notice Dad aging a little. Dad never really got "old" to me, he became more distinguished. His skin never really wrinkled, and his hair was never completely gray.

DAD'S LAST HOLIDAY

Chapter 6

We wanted our children to experience the joy of Mississippi holidays. Many holidays we would return to Mississippi to be with our families. A Mississippi holiday was the best of all. It seemed that for Christmas most people decorated their houses and yards with lights. Even the poorest families did some kind of decorating. Mama would start her Christmas cooking two weeks before Christmas with homemade fruit cakes. After making a large batch, she would make a sample for the family to taste to make sure the flavor and texture was perfect. Dad was the king taster, if he said the sample was perfect Mama would start baking. Mama would line the table with six to ten decorative tin cake pans of different shapes and sizes. Many of the fruit cakes would be given as gifts. As a batch of fruit cakes cooked, Mama would line the tins with foil paper then waxed paper. She would moisten her fruit cakes every few days with a small amount of rum. Each day the house would smell more and more like Christmas. While sitting around watching television, we would be shelling pecans and walnuts. Deserts were all completed two days before Christmas, which left Christmas even for the main meal except turkey, dressing and rolls. The turkey went into the oven by six Christmas morning. The dressing went in by twelve and the rolls thirty minutes before we were ready to eat. As the dressing was cooking, more foods were being heated on the stove while several of us would help set the tables.

Dad was one happy man during this time because his family was together, and love and happiness was in the air. And don't forget the king taster was feasting on almost everything. Mom would have the table covered with cakes and pies. Fruit bowls would be overflowing with apples, oranges, pears, grapes, bananas, nuts, and candy canes from the produce market downtown. The refrigerator would smell like potato salad when you open the door. Boy I can almost smell and taste the food right now.

The tree would be filled with so many gifts that they would overflow pass the tree. Dad would sit in his chair and proudly talk about all of God's blessings on this family. By the weather being so warm in Mississippi, the grandkids would play outside for hours, and constantly come inside for a snack or water. The yard would be filled with so many grandkids that they would attract other kids from the neighborhood. I think Mom and Dad were happy that our home was still considered a fun house by the neighborhood.

As Dad aged and the number of grandkids grew, he started giving each grandkid $5 for Christmas. For some reason the grandkids treated this $5 like $50. Their actions put a smile on Dad's face that was worth a million dollars. On Dad's last Christmas he shared personal feelings with me that touched my heart. He said, "I have so little to give so many. I hope my grandkids remember me for who I am, instead of the $5. I don't have a chance to teach them all I taught you girls, but I did teach them about the Lord. I know I only see your kids a few times a year, but I know you and Lewis are teaching them the right way to go. Barbara Nell lives so far away that I only see them every few years. That's why I am thankful for the telephone and pictures". He paused, and looked around the room at the kids playing. I assured him that we will teach them what he has taught us. He continued, "I hope the grandkids here can see the life I live before them. We take them to church; I just hope they remember what I've been teaching them. Minnie Pearl this world is so wicked. Black folk need to work extra hard to get the same things white folk get. We have to work harder, learn more, do more, baby we just have to be better. I don't think the grandkids know this yet, they don't understand what we have really been though". I explained that as parents we have to make sure they understand the world we live in. They need to know our history, our real history. Dad said," I really don't think they know we are going through something right now. That's why I continue to pray for all of you, and you need to keep praying too. You can never pray too much".

Our last Christmas together was a very special one. Dad had a chance to meet his youngest grandchild, Dontaye Martice Stewart. I tried so hard to have Dontaye on Dad's birthday, July 26th, but Dontaye was born on July 28, 1988. To Dad Dontaye was still special because he was born around his birthday. Not only did he see his youngest grandchild, but also his first great grandchild as well. Andrew Gamal Davis was born on August 28, 1988 by Bobbie Ann' daughter; Eltina Davis.

The house was filled with sounds of kids playing, the smell of Christmas foods cooking, laughter of family, friends and neighbors visiting; and as always the talking of shopping, shopping and more shopping. For some reason Dad just continued to play around with the kids. He was giving Dontaye and Andrew a sample of his wobbly leg ride. They would smile and occasionally laugh as Dad gave each a wobbly leg ride while making a song out of strange sounds. For some reason Dad made an effort to touch or hold each grandkids and Andrew. Now as I look back, he must have known or felt what was to lie ahead. A few days after Christmas Dad developed a kidney infection. I went with Lewis to take Dad to the V.A.

Hospital where he was given medications for a kidney infection and fever. We honestly though Dad was fine, so we decided to leave the following morning before day to return to Illinois.

This was such a good holiday; the month of December was always big for our segment of the family. Nena Unkeyta, our first born turned seventeen on December 16th announced that she would be graduating in June and going to college in the fall. Lewis Kurkie, our middle child turned thirteen on December 14th playfully announced that he would be going to high school in the fall. And, we had a chance to show off our late baby; Dontaye who was only five months old.

Once I returned to work in Illinois, I received a long distance call in the main office that caused my heart to pound. I almost ran to the office, because I had never received a long distance call from Mississippi at work in the past seventeen years of teaching. Bobbie Ann told me that Dad had developed a blood clot, and had passed out. She assured me that he would be just fine, and she wanted me to wait before coming home. Something inside me made me prepare to go home anyway. I made arrangements to go home to Mississippi for two weeks to help care for Dad when he returned home from the hospital.

Flight reservations were made, and I was on my way with Dontaye. Dad wasn't as alert as I thought he would be. As a family, some of us visited Dad three to four times a day; not to mention church members and friends. To my surprise on one visit Dad wasn't truly responding to us, and he didn't ask about Mama. I was visiting along with Albertine, but Dad continued to look out the window as if he was starring at something. He ate a small portion of his food as he continued to stare out the window. Albertine said, "Dad do you know who I am?" He responded, "Yes, Jesus". His eyes were glassy with a bluish grey tint. I had never seen Dad's eyes so light and glassy. Albertine tried to communicate more, "Dad do you know who this is?"Albertine clearly pointed at me. Dad looked at me. Turned and looked out the window and said, "Oh, Jesus". He clearly didn't focus in on me. Albertine and I just stared at each other for about a minute. Our Dad didn't know us. As we discussed what we had observed, we realized that Dad was focusing in on Jesus-The Head of his life.

That Sunday when we returned home, we were in somewhat a sad mood. First, we had too many guests at home, and needed to get to the hospital before visiting hours were over. It felt like they were there to comfort us before anything had happened. Second, I couldn't shake this sad mood I was in, I just couldn't do it. Around 7:00pm I had to let our guest know that some of us had to go back to the hospital to check on Dad. I returned to the hospital with Albertine, and Bobbie Ann.

When we made it to the hospital there was a white hand towel wrapped around Dad's head. Seeing that towel sent cold chills through my body. The attending nurse explained that because the bed couldn't be moved, a towel was placed on Dad's head to protect him from the cold air from the vent above his head. Then I remembered that I had complained about the cold air blowing on his head. Dad was sound asleep, so we didn't disturb him. I tried to tell myself that Dad was tire from all his visitors, but I still had this strange sad mood. The events of the last three days made me feel that Dad felt an eternal presence of the Lord.

For some strange reason I wasn't sleepy that night. As I talked to Bobbie Ann and Albertine they weren't sleepy either. We spent most of the night talking about our childhood, our great parents, and how we must do our best to care for Dad. Although we had looked at a few nursing homes for rehabilitation, we didn't want our father put in a nursing home for fear of him feeling thrown away. We also knew putting Dad in a nursing home would make Mom slowly die.

It was so strange, we were laughing and talking, but we were still very sad. Mom was staying in bed most of the time, she didn't even want to eat or even talk much. We would go back and forth into Mom's bedroom checking on her. She looked at me one time and said, "Albert isn't coming home is he?" I strongly said, "Mom, Dad may have to go to a nursing home first to work on his walking. We need to get him ready to come home. "Minnie", she said as she starred into my eyes; "Albert said that he didn't want to die hungry. Minnie we can't let him die hungry". Mom looked at me with watery eyes, and I knew I had to make every possible attempt to feed Dad on each visit. I sat down in a chair next to Mom's bed and told her everything Dad had for lunch. As I touched Mom's hand I said, "Dad had a good meal for lunch. I ate some of it myself. Dad ate a few spoons of pureed roast beef, mashed potatoes with gravy, half a carton of milk, and he ate a few spoons of pudding. Oh by the way Dad had a bowel movement before I left". Mom just smiled. Then I said, "Mom, why don't you eat so I can tell Dad that you are eating too. She said, "Yes, bring me a little something to eat". I fixed her a small plate of food and took it to her. As she slowly ate her food she looked at me sadly and said, "Minnie, Albert isn't coming home, but he won't die hungry. Promise me you won't let him die hungry". Then I promised that I would do everything I could to make sure Dad wouldn't die hungry.

Returning to the living room; I shared Mom's concern about Dad eating to my sisters. To my surprise she has said the same thing to my other sisters. It was mentioned that Dad had a saying, "I may die poor, but I won't die hungry". We joked about the matter, and how Dad would buy so much grocery. Yes, we always had more than enough food for our family and some to share with others. I believe that we were so blessed because our parents were so willing to give to others.

We spent the whole night telling stories about growing up. We went from one story to another. Bobbie Ann told a story about Mrs. Brown her 4th grade teacher. Bobbie Ann told us that Mrs. Brown was mean, and she wore black and white every day. She even had black and white shoes. Bobbie Ann said, "Mrs. Brown was probably the person that started school uniforms". Mrs. Brown had each student to stand and tell what they had for breakfast that morning. Bobbie Ann stood and said, "I had smothered chicken and gravy, rice, scrambled eggs, buttered toast, orange juice and milk". Mrs. Brown said, "Bobbie Ann you know you didn't have all that for breakfast. That's what you eat on Sundays. What did you really have?" Bobbie Ann repeated the same thing. Mrs. Brown was so upset with Bobbie Ann that she had her to stand in the corner. Bobbie Ann couldn't understand why she was punished for telling the truth. When she made it home she told Mom and Dad. Mrs. Brown heard from Mom that following morning. Mom took a cab to the school that morning, and had a talk with Mrs. Brown in front of the class. Mrs. Brown gladly apologized to Bobbie Ann in front of the class. Mrs. Lela Mae put her purse strap on her shoulder, put her head up and walked out the door. Bobbie Ann said Mrs. Brown never picked at her again.

Albertine told a story about Betty Jean, our second cousin on Dad's side of the family. Early one spring Dad was cleaning the yard. Dad had started a small brush fire in the back yard to burn yard debris from the winter. Dad said, "Girls, please don't play in the fire. You can look at it, but you can't play in it". There were so many fun things to do that Albertine didn't want to be around the fire.

Dad's mom, Mama Lula was visiting with her two great grandkids, Betty Jean and Brother. Mom was in the kitchen with Mama Lula cooking up a feast. Some neighborhood kids were over playing with us, and Dad was busy cleaning the yard. Mom had taken our hair down to wash after we ate. Albertine's hair was long and wavy. As we played Albertine's hair stood out more and more on her head. Finally, we stopped playing and decided to stand around the fire. Dad had us to stand a long way from the fire, as he continued to glance over at us. Betty Jean, of all people, decided to poke a stick in the fire. Albertine said, "No Betty no, Dad said don't play in the fire". Betty Jean wouldn't stop. As Albertine was going to tell Dad; just that moment Betty Jean took the stick out the fire. As she did, it passed Albertine's head as her hair started to blaze up. Albertine started to run and scream. Family members started to run to see what was happening. Poor Dad tried but he couldn't control Albertine, so Mama took her dish water and dashed it on Albertine's head. She also emptied the salt box on her head too. Poor Albertine's head looked like a plucked chicken. There wasn't much Mom and Dad could do at that time to make things better for Albertine other than hugs and words of reassurance. Mom and Dad shaved Albertine's head to check for burns, and speed up hair growth. This was really a hard time for Albertine because kids would tease her about a light birthmark on her face, her stuttering and now her ball head. Dad tried to assure Albertine that she was still a pretty little girl. Mom spent time each day massaging Albertine's scalp. Look like the hair just started to grow. In about a month and a half, Albertine's hair was growing nicely. A matter of fact her hair was long by summer. Not once did our family laugh or make Albertine feel ugly; it was just the opposite.

I told a story about how Mama stopped me from killing George Lambus, our play brother. Mama had made me the prettiest pink dress with ruffles. I took great care in not getting it dirty. Mama let me ware my dress the last day of vacation bible school. This was the day we had our end of vacation bible school program. I was really feeling good about myself; I did well in the program, and I looked good too. I don't know why, but that George Lambus just had to mess with me of all people. Would you believe that George Lambus pushed me into a ditch of standing muddy water? I couldn't believe it; my dress, socks, shoes, slip, and panties were muddy too. The people that said I looked good, were now laughing and pointing at me. Before I knew it, I had said I was going to kill that George Lambus. I knew I had to pay him back. My best way to get him back was with surprise attack.

As kids walked home from vacation bible school; I was laying in wait in a large old oak tree in the corner of our front yard; with a long board in my hands. Looking in the group, there he was. The group started to get smaller as kids went in the direction of their homes. As he got closer I positioned my board high over my right shoulder. Just as I was about to let George Lambus have it, I heard a high pitched piercing voice, "No Minnie, no Minnie, don't kill him". By that time George Lambus looked up directly into my eyes. He knew I was some mad. He took off running like a rabbit. I guess you can say; Mama saved the day, or a life. After so much talking it was morning, but it was still black dark outside. Albertine went to bed at her home next door, but Bobbie Ann and I stayed in the living room watching television. At some point I fell asleep, but was awaken by a strange telephone ring. I jumped up and answered the phone before the second ring.

"Hello", I said. The voice on the line said, "This is the V.A. Hospital. May I speak to Mrs. Smith?" I said, "No, please! My mother is ill, I'll take the message". Before the person on the line could give me the message; Mom said, "It's about Albert, isn't it?" By that time everyone in the house was awaken. The person on the line continued, "Mr. Smith passed away in his sleep this morning". I didn't know what to say, or what to do. The only words that came were, "Thank you, I'll tell my mother". If I said something else I don't remember. As I looked at Bobbie Ann she said, "Oh no!" By that time Albertine was in the living room too. She explained how she went to bed after leaving us but couldn't sleep well. She went on to say, "I had butterflies in my stomach that gave me diarrhea. I woke up at least three times last night. You know, I felt something was going to happen, I just didn't know what". Bobbie just stared at Albertine, then at me. Bobbie Ann quickly agreed that she also had a strange feeling last night, that made her not want to sleep in her bed. Maybe we all felt in a strange way that Dad was leaving us, maybe we didn't want to say it. Only Mama said it out loud.

Making telephone calls was a very difficult thing to do. How could we let Barbara Nell know about Dad? She was so far away to receive news of this magnitude. We just started going through the motion of making calls. I called Barbara Nell, as the others started making other calls to family members, the pastor and very close friends.

I then turned my attention to Mama, and what we needed to do for her. "Mama", I said, "Are you alright"? She looked at me with a blank stare and said, "Albert is gone, I just knew he would never come home. Minnie, Albert knew he would never come home too, I don't know what I am going to do, or what is going to happen to this family. The man of this family is gone, Albert is gone". I had to let Mama express her feelings. Mom was trying to be strong for the family, but she needed to let her feeling go. Mom hadn't really cried, she just wanted to check on us, and tell us what needed to be done. In less than an hour the house was filled with relatives and friends. Barbara Nell made the earliest reservations she could, and was there within two days. In my mind I could only think; Dad is gone. On February 2, 1989 my Dad went home. How can I say goodbye? Mom needs her girls by her side as we go through this process.

As preparations were made for the funeral, the days just flew by. A day before the services, Dr. Rev S.L. Spann called Mom to make a request. One of Dad's military friends from over forty five years ago wanted to speak. Mom explained that Dad's life spoke for itself, and that's why she didn't want a long drawn out service. She did decide to let this man speak, but only if he could limit it to two minutes. Later that day we received a plant from Mexico. News does travel fast and far.

On the day of the services I truly understood what Mom meant when she said, "Dad's life spoke for itself". The cards and many acts of kindness were unbelievable. There Mama was, with her four girls and a large host of other relatives. Dad's military buddy did have encouraging words to say; it's too sad that he didn't take the time to tell my Dad. Dad's friend told how Dad had tried to talk to them about gambling off their monthly earnings, constantly drinking and being so loud. Instead, he wanted them to save most of their money so they would have a nest egg when they got out of the military. Dad also talked to them about respect and their bad language. Most importantly, Dad talked to them about God and his saving grace. Dad wanted them to see that they should be thankful for each day that they were still alive and still whole. This man acknowledged that Dad was right, but he was having too much fun for God. He wanted the family to know that what Dad said, and how he carried himself did impact his life. Dad's many sayings did stay with him, and were part of his foundation for his Christian life style.

I know this is a strange thing to say; "This was a very sad day, but it was also a very clamming day". Mrs. Watkins of the Mississippi Mass Choir did a selection as Mrs. Lannie Spann McBride accompanied her on the piano. Mrs. Watkins did an arrangement of Yes Jesus Loves Me. After service, we traveled down the highway to the family cemetery. I had Mom to look back at what looked like endless headlights following us. Mom smiled as motorcycle officers blocked the intersection as we came through. Mom said in her soft voice, "Albert really deserves military honors and all of this. He really does".

When we returned home the house was filled with relatives and friends. Mrs. Miller, our neighbor and family friend, had prepared a feast. Not to mention all the other foods from church members, friends, and relatives. Mom really didn't want to eat; she just wanted to rest in bed for a while.

As it started to get dark, a cold frost moved in. The temperature dropped and it started to rain. This was a cold, bone chilling rain. Lewis kept up with the weather reports, and decided that we had better leave first thing in the morning. So, we packed and decided to get rest to be ready for travel by 5:00 am.

We were awakened by a loud cracking sound. As we looked outside, we could hear more cracking sounds. It was so strange, it was black dark outside. There were no street lights anywhere. The only houses with lights were Mom's house and Albertine's house. The radio report stated that a massive ice storm was headed that way, and the city may be immobile for days. As we checked on family members, we were told all of northwest Jackson was without lights. Several electrical transformers had been damaged by falling trees. Police with spot lights were checking each street for down power lines. Even the police couldn't explain how it was possible for these two houses to have lights. Later we found out that the power lines for the street were also down. Mom said, "As always Albert is still protecting us". As a science teacher; according to scientific principles these lights being on is impossible. But, through God I called it a Miracle.

Within thirty minutes we had the car loaded. I quickly packed finger foods, fruits and something to drink. It was hard telling Mom and my three sisters goodbye, but we had to beat the ice storm. A matter of fact we left during the storm. As Lewis was slowly driving up Highway 55, I was praying and talking to God. Trees were partly on the highway, trucks and cars had run off the highway. There we were driving on ice; Lewis said we could only stop for gas around Memphis. It took over six hours to travel one hundred and ninety two miles. My toes were numb for partly putting on "my brakes" as Lewis was driving. My body was just tired. The kids mostly slept through it all. When I saw rain in Memphis, I just had to give God a big thank you at that point.

I never thought I could let Dad go. Deep inside I thought I would always have my dad, and that I'll always be his little girl. Leaving in an ice storm made me feel like I left so much behind, and that I will never feel that secure feeling again. While thanking God for the life he had given me, I realized that I wasn't really alone. God was there for me. Looking around the van was my supportive husband, and three loving healthy children. I knew everything was going to be alright. In the mist of sorrow and life's difficulties there were invisible hands helping me as I travel through this phase of my life. With all these wonderful memories, I know my Dad will always be with me. Dad believed in thanking God for giving us to him; I thank God for giving us the World Greatest Dad.

I returned to Mississippi on March 25, 1989 for Easter break. I just needed and wanted to spend time with Mom. Mama was going through a phase of depression. She wouldn't go in the kitchen, or even watch TV. She was avoiding things she enjoyed with Dad. She only opened the front door to check the mail.

We talked about Dad, and how he wouldn't want her to live like this. I said, "Mom what do you want to do?" She said, "Minnie you don't understand. I lost my best friend, the father of my children, my lover and my provider. I lived with Albert longer than I lived with Ma and Pa".

Holding her hands I said, "Mom I am so sorry. Please tell me how you feel inside. What do you want to do?" Mom looked at me and around the room. I guess she wanted to make sure we were still alone in the house. Softly she said, "I want to scream". I said, "Scream Mama". As she started to scream, I Said, "Scream, scream Mama, scream". Mama screamed that day until she couldn't scream anymore. It was that day that my Mom started coming out of her depression. She took a bath; put on a skirt and blouse, not another gown. She went into the kitchen and made a pot of Folgers coffee, as she put on a pot of water for grits. Out of the blue she said, "Are my stories on?" Thank God, Mama is back.

FAMILY LOVE

Chapter 7

Bobbie Ann, Barbara Nell, Minnie Pearl and Albertine

A family that truly has love is a beautiful union to behold. Within a family love can help it members deal with sorrow, hurt and even death. I was blessed with a family that just didn't say they loved each other, they lived it. My father's side of the family was small and distant.

Dad's parents were Lula (Odell) and Cebe Watts Smith; this union gave birth to eleven children, but only three lived past the age of one.

- Lula Ann didn't marry or have children
- Alberta's and Lieutenant Harris' union gave birth to Margaret
- Albert's first union with Mae Lola (Adams) gave birth to Robert;

Second union with Lela Mae gave birth to Bobbie Ann, Barbara Nell, Albertine and Minnie Pearl

1. Bobbie Ann's and Leon Davis'union gave birth to Marnetta, Maurice, Tony Fitzgerald and Eltina
2. Barbara Nell's
   1st union with Sam Yusef Velaidan gave birth to Dino;
   2nd union with Larry Galloway gave birth to Trava;
   3rd union with Kent Dias gave birth to Kentra
3. Albertine's and James Sutton's union gave birth to Felicia Diana
4. Minnie Pearl's and Lewis C. Stewart's union gave birth to Nena Unkeyta, Lewis Kurkie, and Dontaye Martice

Mom's parents were Minnie Lee (Kitchen) and John "West" Ervin; this union gave birth to ten children. Mom had three brothers and six sisters.

- Aunt Ella's (Eva) and Uncle William Berrage's union gave birth to Freddie Ray and Willie James
- Mom-Lela Mae's (Sister) and Dad-Albert Smith's union gave birth to Bobbie Ann, Barbara Nell, Albertine and Minnie Pearl.

1. Bobbie Ann's and Leon Davis'union gave birth to Marnetta, Maurice, Tony Fitzgerald and Eltina
2. Barbara Nell's
   1st union with Sam Yusef Velaidan gave birth to Dino;
   2nd union with Larry Galloway gave birth to Trava;
   3rd union with Kent Dias gave birth to Kentra
3. Albertine's and James Sutton's union gave birth to Felicia Diana
4. Minnie Pearl's and Lewis C. Stewart's union gave birth to Nena Unkeyta, Lewis Kurkie, and Dontaye Martice

- Aunt Thelma's and Uncle Walter Perkins' union gave birth to Curtis
- Uncle John Wesley's (Buddy) and Aunt Doreather (Perkins') union gave birth to Maxine, Annie Ruff, John Wesley, Shirley Ann, Carrie Mae, and Mary Ann
- Aunt Mae Bell's and Uncle Charlie Washington's union gave birth to Mae Pearl and Jerry Dean

- Uncle Wadie Hamp's (Ginn) and Aunt Louise (Adam's) union gave birth to Wadie Hamp
- Aunt Mary's (Fenen) and Uncle Wardell Proctor's union gave birth to Nadean, Curtis Wesley (Dub), Linda, David, Gregory, and Manuel
- Aunt Louise's (Litton) and Uncle Tommie (T. C.) Burnett's union gave birth to Tommie Cene and Eddie Lewis
- Aunt Dorothy's (Baby) and Uncle Arthur Washington's union gave birth to Arthur Clifford (AC), George, Jessie, Diane, Debra, Tommie, Willie, Eric and Melvin
- Uncle Walter James' (Jack) and Aunt Ann (Hobson's) union gave birth to Minnie, Pearlean (Hobson), and Earlean (Hobson)

I had so many cousins, that I never knew how many I really had. All I knew was no matter what games we wanted to play, there were always enough kids to play. The family came together so often you didn't have to notify the whole group, just a few and the rest knew to come together. We were together for Christmas, Thanksgiving, Easter, 4th of July, Labor Day, Memorial Day, weddings, funerals, harvest time, family reunions and many 1st Sundays of the month. Someone would mention a reason and they would come together; food, fun and all. This practice still goes on today.

When we came together there were all kinds of foods like hen and dressing, fried chicken, ham, greens, peas, corn, cornbread, candied yams, assorted deserts, the list goes on. A many times we would have a fish fry or barbeque, and say bring your favorite dish. It was fun learning how to help prepare and cook different foods, not to mention the sampling. I also enjoyed playing with my sisters and cousins. We even had other people there with more kids.

What I remembered the most was the warm feeling I had inside as I shared in the love of my family. No matter what situation arose; the family was there to share in love, joy, happiness, sorrow, and pain. There were always hugs, kisses, and handshakes. The elders would pass down words of wisdom and knowledge. There was always a reference to God, and keeping the family together. Today the family leaders have changed, but the theme remains the same. With God and love we can keep this family bond strong and together. Our family reunion banner theme is, "BONDED BY LOVE".

Mama and Daddy made sure our segment of this family was strong. Dad's life style gained him the respect of our neighborhood, surrounding neighborhoods, religious leaders, business leaders, Black and White alike. He gave respect, and received respect in return. We did things as a family. Fussing and fighting was a definite "no". If we were caught fussing or fighting we would get a long lecture on family, love and God's view. After all that, we would have to make up with, "I am sorry" and a big hug too. By the time Dad was done lecturing; we would have forgotten what started the problem in the first place. Believe me; we learned to solve disagreements without fussing and fighting. Thinking back now, maybe Dad was using reverse psychology on us. Well, what do you know; it worked.

We had family outings like the movies, zoo, state fair, or just going downtown to Farish Street to buy hot tamales, warm roasted peanuts, ice cream from The Hole In The Wall, and get hot buttered popcorn. Sometimes Mama would cook foods to take with us; like fried chicken, and tea cakes or cookies. It was just good quality family time.

My brother Robert was old enough to be my father. Robert's mother died when he was young; Mama Lula helped Dad to raise Robert. I remember Robert only as an adult. When I was around five Robert came home from the army for a visit. I was so happy to see him and he was happy to see me. Robert would pay me a nickel to put in my piggy bank for taking his military boots off. I received much love, and many nickels from proudly helping take Robert's boots off. As a teenager I learned that Dad was twelve years older than Mom, and Mom was twelve years older than Robert. Robert coming to visit was always a celebration and a feast with family and friends.

I loved my sisters so much that I could feel their pain or humiliation. I was my sister Albertine's protector. Albertine was one year older than I, but my personality was much stronger and outgoing. Albertine was born with a slight speech problem and a light patch birthmark over her right eye. Kids use to call her map face because her birthmark was shaped like the U.S. map. Albertine had problems with some "S", "Q" and "Z" words. Can you picture telling somebody off when you might not be able to use the words you need to tell them off with? I would step in every chance I got to defend Albertine; why should she be picked at because of what God had given her. By the time we were in Jr. High, kids had stopped picking at Albertine.

When Dad's twin sister, Aunt Alberta, died; my cousins came to live with us. Betty Jean was my age, but very big boned. At fourteen Betty Jean wore a size eleven shoe, and was 5ft. 10ins. tall. Arthur (Brother) was small for a twelve year old. Brother wasn't even five feet tall. Mama went on a mission to make Betty Jean clothes for her age, and that would make her look smaller. Mama also worked on Betty Jean's manners and how she acted. Betty Jean would walk up behind Mom and say "Boo" or tickle her. Can you imagine five feet two inches Mama having Betty Jean doing this to her several times a day. Mama motivation was that if she could help Betty Jean look better maybe she would act better. Mama worked overtime on this mission. Betty Jean soon started looking and acting like a fourteen year old girl. With open arms our family had grown by two.

Bobbie Ann married young. Mama and Daddy had to sign to let her get married. Bobbie Ann and Leon Davis married at Pastor Roberts' home on Bailey Ave. The family embraced Leon as a member of the family.

Our big sister Bobbie Ann needed our love and support when she grieved the death of her son; Maurice. Bobbie Ann was and still is a loving mother. When Marnetta was born she showed that she could be a mother like Mom. I had so much so much fun holding and feeding Marnetta that I gave her the nickname Binky. Would you believe I got the name from a pacifier? Marnetta is called Binky to this day. Maurice was Bobbie Ann's second child; and first son. Maurice didn't grow as fast as Mom felt he should. Dr. Lyford told Bobbie Ann and Leon to continue to feed and nurture him. Bobbie Ann, Mama and Aunt Fenen went in full force to nurture Maurice. He appeared to be happy, but never rolled over or crawled.

After Maurice's death Dr. Lyford told Bobbie Ann and Leon that he was so sorry for their lost. He knew Maurice was sick, but he wanted Bobbie Ann to enjoy each day she would have with Maurice. Dr. Lyford explained that Maurice was born with an enlarged liver that would continue to grow at a faster rate than the rest of his body. He was expected to live only one or two months. As Maurice thrived, Dr. Lyford became more reluctant to tell them that Maurice was going to die, and there was no medical treatment for his condition.

Maurice's funereal was so sad. To me even the sky was crying. The funereal was small with family and very close friends. He was buried in the country with other family members under a big maple tree. It rained so hard that day that the little grave filled with water. Grandpa decided to put the coffin in the church, and bury Maurice the following morning. This church was special to our family, because Grandpa help build this church. Family members said Grandpa did most of the work on the church along with Jacks' help.

Bobbie Ann loosing Maurice caused her to open up to Mom and Dad about things that were happening in her marriage. Leon had become abusive and jealous. He didn't want her to wear her hair down, wear certain clothes; he didn't even want her to talk to certain people. He had also started drinking and staying out at night. Bobbie Ann said, "The night Maurice died; Leon was out with his friends drinking. When he did make it home; there she was crying in shock holding a dead baby. Instead of comforting his wife, he took off running to his mother's house". Things started to make sense as to why one of Leon's family members came over to notify us about Maurice, and not Leon. We had a telephone, and Bobbie Ann and Leon did too; Leon could have call Mom or Dad. After hearing the news we were at Bobbie Ann's in less than thirty minutes.

Leon started drinking more and more. He started ignoring his family. He had become verbally and physically abusive to Bobbie Ann. Bobbie Ann couldn't take it anymore; she decided to move back home with Marnetta. Dad made it clear to Bobbie Ann that she was welcome to come home at any time, and that they wouldn't influence her decision.

I want you to understand why I am shared this information with you. My parents could have gone to Leon with chose words in anger, but they didn't. Our male cousins could have beaten him to death, but they didn't. Dad did it God's way. Dad was the one that talked to Leon. I don't know what he said to Leon, but afterward we saw a changed person. Leon continued to come over to talk to Dad while having a cup of coffee, and to check on Bobbie Ann. After many months, Bobbie Ann decided to take the new Leon back. It was family love shown by Mom and Dad that allowed Leon to move in our home with Bobbie Ann. Love is forgiving.

The best show of family love was shared with me by Aunt Litton. Aunt Litton is now eighty seven years old, and the last of Mom's siblings. This story of family is deep and funny. Aunt Litton explained how love for a sister or brother can be so deep that it hurts to be separated. It's even harder when you go through life doing almost everything together. Aunt Litton and Aunt Fenen grew up like twins; they were eleven months and a few weeks apart. Aunt Litton went on to say, "I loved Fenen so much that I couldn't let her go." "What do you mean", I said. "Minnie I remember it clearly", she said. I listened as she continued to share how deep her love was for Aunt Fenen. She said, "Wardell came to the field one day while we were working. Wardell ask Pa to let him marry Fenen. Pa said yes, and Fenen said yes too. I started to cry. I cried the rest of the day. I even cried when they got married. I was crying so much that in a few days Wardell and Fenen came back to get me and take me with them". I said, "I know Uncle Wardell didn't come back to get you?" She said, "Yes he did, and I stayed a few days with then at his mother's and grandmother's house. Then Wardell took me over to Sister's house in Jackson. After a few more days Pa sent my cousin Tommie Ervin to bring me back to the country". Well if that isn't family love, I don't know what is.

HELPING HANDS OF LOVE

Chapter 8

Top: Aunt Fenen, Aunt Litton;
seated: Aunt Baby, Mama, and Aunt Thelma

Some decisions are hard to make. You have to pray about them before you step out on your own. One of the hardest decisions I have ever had to make was; how could I help my sisters care for my mother while living almost eight hundred miles away? Money will only do so much. Also, in the back of my mind was the quantity and quality of time I would be missing if I remained in Illinois. We had already talked about maybe moving back to be near our families. Lewis Kurkie had already moved to Jackson in 1998 to attend Jackson State University while majoring in Marketing and Advertising. Since I am a detailed person, I decided to apply for my Teachers License for Mississippi. Just having it wouldn't hurt.

My life changed on Oct 15, 1999 when I had a thymoma removed. I fully recovered after surgery, having one round of chemo and twenty six radiation treatments. Our lives changed even more when Lewis' mother died on November 8, 1999 in Canton, Mississippi. My dear friend and neighbor; Francis Coe took care of me while Lewis, Nena and Dontaye were away in Canton. I was in no condition to travel. Francis was my white neighbor that lived in front of us, and Dontays' play grandmother. Dontaye even took Francis to school in 4ᵗʰ grade for Grandparents Day. Frances was the one that took care of me when the family traveled to Mississippi to funeralize Lewis' mother.

You can say Francis was my helping hands. Each morning I would shower, dress, and come down stairs. I would open the door so Francis could come in when she made it there. Francis would care for me like I was her daughter. She would come early in the morning after taking care of her dog, and would go home for the night around eight. We mainly talked, watch TV and shared life stories. After meeting Mom one time they became lifelong telephone friends. Francis was even willing to move to Mississippi with me to help care for Mom.

I remember Dad saying, "Why take something to the alter to pray about; then take it back with you? You suppose to take it to the alter and leave it. Let God deal with it", and that's what I did. I gave it to God. I went through this illness with very few people knowing about it, or even bringing the wrong spirits around me. I would lie on the floor in front of the fireplace and read the bible, meditate and talk to God. This illness took me to a higher level in my Christian life. I also felt that God was getting me ready for something; I was willing to wait on his directions.

I still didn't know what God had gotten me ready for. I was faithfully working in the church, working with students before and after school free, doing outreach and taking care of my family. I started to feel better and get my energy back. I eagerly waited on my six week checkup.

I remember once during my illness taking back my problem and dealing with it. God never let me know to take chemo. A team of eight doctors studied my case because this tumor was so rare. Dr. Myers told me that within a normal surgeon's life, he will never remove a thymoma. He informed me that on the team seven doctors said no chemo, but radiation was needed because of cutting and the possibility of one or more cells being left behind. He went on to say that only one doctor said to have chemo. Dr. Myers was going to leave this decision up to me and Lewis. I prayed about it and didn't feel anything from God on the matter. I didn't realize God had sent me a team to give me my answer; yes the team of seven. From a biblical standpoint think of the number seven. Yes that phase of the recovery was complete. My surgery went very well. My body was healthy. I never smoked or drank. I was only taking medication for an underactive thyroid. Also, I wouldn't be taking any medication related to this illness. Isn't God good?

Thinking about Dontaye, I went ahead of God. I decided to take chemo to improve my chances of being here with Dontaye as he grew up. I decided to take chemo. I intravenously took three drugs back to back; they were Cis-Platinum, Adriamycin, and Cytoxan. When I walked out the treatment center I felt like my muscles were shaking on my bones. Those drugs almost killed me; I was vomiting and having diarrhea at the same time. I had a fear of putting anything in my body; thinking the vomiting and diarrhea to start up again. In the back of my mind I continued to think of the number seven. I wasn't this sick or weak when I had surgery. Thank God for helping me get back on track. I decided not to have another round of chemo, that was nineteen years ago. Dontaye is now twenty nine years old with a five year son D.J.

On spring break while I was visiting Lewis Kurkie and the rest of the family; I decided to apply for teacher certification in Mississippi. I took all the necessary paperwork with me; thinking that maybe in a few weeks my license would be mailed to me. Things didn't happen that way.

While applying I was asked, "Do you have your test score on your Teacher Certification Exam"? I said, "No I don't. I know my test score was high because of my student teachers' assignment and qualifying to teach in Illinois after graduation". After going into a file room, she came back and said, "When did you do your student teaching"? I said, "I did my student teaching the spring of 1970". She said, "Where did you do your student teaching"? I said," I did my student teaching at Central High School". She looked at me and said, "Where"? I looked at her and said, "Central High School, old Central High School". She quickly went into a different room. After about fifteen minutes, she returned and said, "We are working on it; give us a little more time". I waited another fifteen minutes. Then she walked out with two other ladies. She looked at me with a smile and said, "Mrs. Stewart you don't have to wait for your license. If you did your student teaching here at Central High your score had to be high. Mrs. Stewart your license is for high school Chemistry and Biology; Mrs. Stewart welcome to Mississippi". Before I knew it I said, "Thank God; I thought I had to wait". She said, "No, with your qualifications you don't have to wait". She handed me the license, and I walked out the door telling everyone to have a blessed day. When I made it outside I almost ran to the car screaming and showing Bobbie Ann the license.

The summer of 2000 I returned to Mississippi to help care for Mama. I had to fight for her. I prayed about it, talked to Pastor Namon Klines about it, and talked to Lewis about it. It was shown to me that God had to get my body healthy to help care for Mama. In hindsight, I can see how things just lined up. I had a teaching position before moving to Mississippi; while some teachers were waiting for their assignment. I leased a four bedroom house based on Lewis Kurkie's recommendations that was only five minutes from Mom's house. Dontaye's school worked out, and I got involve with my old church. I was home.

The greatest show of love was during Mama's illness. When illness strikes, you don't know all the other unrelated sorrows, pain or hardships you might have to face at that same time. My Mom's three sisters were so loving and caring toward each other that they took it upon themselves to fight with Mama. Their actions showed unconditional love. Aunt Thelma had recovered from abdominal cancer just a few years earlier, but still had a heart condition. Aunt Baby had recovered from a stroke, a mastectomy, and was living with rheumatoid arthritis. Aunt Litton was gaining her life back after helping her college age granddaughter, Jamilla, battle Leukemia for the second time. With all they had faced, they started focusing their attention on Mom. They became her helping hands.

Mom's sisters were so faithful and loving in the way they helped us care for Mama. A many mornings one or two of them would be at Mama's as early as 5:30 a.m. This wasn't just one day a week, sometimes as many as three or five days a week. They would spend most of their time sitting, talking, grooming and even singing with Mama. One day as

I was cooking, I heard harmonizing sounds. As I followed the sounds to Mama's room my soul was touched. Mama and Aunt Baby were singing as both reached upward. My heart was overjoyed to see that even sickness didn't stop their praise.

There were times when Aunt Litton would cook something that Mama had a taste for. Mama would really perk up on those days. In Black culture, food and fellowship are signs of unity and love. Every Friday the family came together at Mama's house. We never had a set menu; we just cooked what we wanted. Most Fridays we knew we would have some kind of fried fish, chicken, greens or cabbage, macaroni and cheese, assorted deserts, lemonade or ice tea; not to mention anything anybody wanted to bring. Many Friday evenings between three and seven we would have as many as fifteen or more family members or friends to stop by. Look like Fridays were always good for Mama; because we had family, friends, food and fellowship.

In January after one of our fellowships ended in sorrow. Aunt Thelma wanted to spend the full weekend with Mama. We had such a great time. Aunt Thelma laughed and joked as we had never seen before. We stayed in the living room until after ten o'clock; as they talked about growing up, being teenagers and just life in general. They didn't want to go to bed; they just couldn't get enough of each other. There was something special about this day, the fellowship, this sharing of love. The following morning was the same. Aunt Thelma was so happy, it was as if she was about to receive the most valuable gift of a life time. Whatever the reason; the fellowship and love were heavenly.

Mama and Aunt Thelma departed with, "I love you". I couldn't put my finger on it, but for some reason this departure was different. Maybe it was the way they stared into each other's eyes, the loving smiles, the gentle good bye kiss or was it the way they said, "I love you"? Whatever it was, it left a mark on the hearts of all of us. Maybe God had given us something to hold on to.

Three days later we were sitting around talking to Mama about our wonderful weekend with Aunt Thelma. When the phone rang we stopped talking, and starred at Mama. This call was different in some strange way. As Bobbie Ann answered the phone, she looked around at the rest of us with a blank stare. She said, "Tommie Cene and Jessie are taking Aunt

Thelma to St. Dominic's Hospital because she is having chest pains". Within fifteen minutes there was another call from Tommie Cene, my Aunt Thelma was gone. How could this happen so fast? We didn't have a chance to say good bye.

Aunt Litton and Aunt Baby; oh my, what are they going to do? They are together all the time. Aunt Thelma and Aunt Litton live next door to each other, while Aunt Baby is only five minutes away. They are known as the three Ervin sisters in their small community. Poor Mama just continued to say, "She tried to tell me, she tried to tell me. All weekend she was trying to tell me good bye. I am so thankful we said we loved each other. She was so happy, and so at peace. In Thelma's own way she did say good bye".

Mama went into a silent no eating, sad phase. As a diabetic, Mama had to eat. Mama's sugar level was dropping, as her blood pressure was rising. We had no choice; Mama had to go to the hospital. The timing was bad, but we couldn't let the family lose two sisters at the same time. To help Mama cope during the funeral, I stayed at the hospital with her while the rest of my sisters went to the funeral. There Mama was with an IV in her arm, a catheter and lying flat on her back. Aunt Mae Bell was in Los Angeles and medically unable to fly. Mama and Aunt Mae Bell talked by phone to each other during the full time of the funeral. Aunt Thelma would have been proud of her sisters and how they talked about their good times, bad times and everlasting love for each other in a way that unconditional.

As days passed, Mama silently grieved. Mama's vital signs were stabilized, but she wasn't eating on her own. As the doctor met with us, he made it clear that Mama needed a feeding tube if she was going to survive at home. How can things change so fast? How can a person be walking, talking and eating one week; then two weeks later be on a feeding tube and in a hospital bed? With God's help we will do whatever is necessary to help improve Mama's quality of life.

This family had just lost one family members, we were not ready or willing to lose another one. Bobby Ann, Albertine and I came up with a schedule that would have someone at Mama's house all the time. We even hired a friend and neighbor to do some sitting for us so we could go to church, or run errands. We tried to make things as close to normal as possible. Our Friday fellowships topped our list. We didn't know how much time Mama had left, so with God's help we had to make each day worth living. We all pitched in to care for Mama, because in this family love conquers all.

It was amazing to see how this family could work together for the love of a family member. No one had to be told what to do; we just did whatever needed to be done. Laundry was done daily as needed, meals were started by any family member, and Mama's physical and personal care was by us girls. We also had help of a CNA twice a week.

With the care given by this family, Mama's health far exceeded the level of improvement expected by her doctor. She went from four feeding tube meals a day to eating four small meals of lightly seasoned soul food a day. She went from not watching TV at all, to keeping up with day time soap operas, and a few family movies. She went from talking very little, to talking constantly as well as singing. Mama's quality of life was gradually coming back, along with love of friends and family she will continue to improve. As always Fridays were very special. This house was filled with laughter, family stories, kids at play, cooking and eating of traditional soul foods. Every Friday was like a holiday. Usually there were several people cooking in the kitchen, as people continued to come in and check on Mama. Sure Mama had her good days and her bad days. But Mama's good days far exceeded her bad days.

Mama's quality of life did improve to some degree, but I could tell she was missing Aunt Thelma. This is one concern that I couldn't help her with; but I could be there for a gentle touch, a talk, or just being there in her room. Daily we had talks with Barbara Nell about Mama's condition, and Barbara Nell talked daily to Mama to let her know she loved her.

Barbara Nell was calling each day, but still felt she needed to see Mom for herself. Barbara Nell's job at UPS only wanted to give her two weeks off. Barbara Nell planned to visit Mom November 14th to November 30th. After reservations were made, Mom became ill. Mom started to eat less and sleep more. The shock came when Mom passed black feces. The black feces was of great concern because Mom was on Coumadin a blood thinner. After a call to her doctor, he suggested that we bring her into the emergency room. I rode in the ambulance with Mom, while Bobbie Ann and Albertine drove. Here we are back at St. Dominic Hospital. The family was just here a few months ago with Aunt Thelma. Mom was checked and quickly put in intensive care. Mom's blood was too thin. Mom had been losing blood around her feeding tube site into her stomach. She was given platelets to thicken her blood. Mom's condition was very serious. Two days later Mom was put in a critical care room, but it didn't look good.

Barbara Nell was concern about Mama being in the hospital, and wanted to change her ticket. We assured her that the platelets were working, and Mom's clotting factor had improved. A few days later Barbara Nell arrived, and was brought to the hospital directly from the airport. I could tell that Mom was happy to see Barbara Nell. She didn't talk much, but constantly looked around at the four of us and just smiled.

In the days to follow Mom was showered with love from family and friends. There were so many people visiting that they brought in more chairs for the room. At all times; one, two or all of us would be there 24/7. On Tuesday November 26 all four of us were at the hospital. Since Albertine had been there all morning, she decided to go home. Mom was sleeping, so I told Barbara Nell and Bobbie Ann that I would spend the night. Barbara Nell said, "No I want to stay; I want to spend as much time as I can with Mom". As we were discussing our schedule the nurse came in and said, "Mrs. Smith's breathing has slowed, If you want to call your family, it's time". We said, "Thank you". I went over to the phone and called Albertine. As she answered the phone: I said, "Albertine, Mom isn't feeling fell; we need you to come back to the hospital". She said, "Okay". Within fifteen minutes Albertine was there. Many other calls were made to family and the pastor. As Mom's four girls surrounded her bed, she slowly passed away. It was such a peaceful transition that the nurse had to tell us she was gone. With peace and humbleness our Mom slept away.

As family and friends gathered in a designated area we were very sad. Aunt Litton and Aunt Baby were very hurt that they didn't make it there in time. Here we are in the same place facing death again. It had only been a few months ago that we were here for Aunt Thelma. Someone in the group said, "It's just like Aunt Sister, She even knew when to die". They were right; this was two days before Thanksgiving.

Mom's home going was sad, but it was a celebration that was in the form of a musical tribute. Mom's love of music made it proper and fitting to celebrate her life in this way. First born granddaughter, Marnetta McIntyre sang, "Bridge Over Troubled Waters". Granddaughter Eltina Davis sang, "Jesus Is My Strength" and "Safe In His Arms", while her nephew Rev. David Proctor sang, "His Eye Is On The Sparrow". Mrs. Mosie Burks of The Mississippi Mass Choir Sang, "When I Get To Heaven" before the eulogy. I truly understand the meaning of "Let your life speak for itself"; Mom's and Dad's lives did just that.

Aunt Louise "Litton" Burnett (91 yrs. old) is Mom's only living sibling.

She is showered with love and great respect;
we are "BONDED IN LOVE".

A LIFE TO REMEMBER

Chapter 9

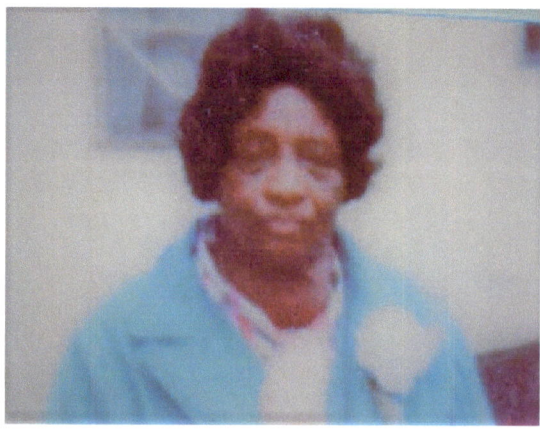

The lives of our elders are the blueprints for the young; this in itself is the passing down of wisdom. If you don't remember the good in a person's life, then there is nothing to build on or pass along. God has given each of us a purpose in life. Our job is to find, or become aware of our purpose as we travel life's journey. We are never alone; there are watchful eyes from above, and countless helping hands along life's journey. I can definitely say that God has used my parents to be helping hands for me and countless others.

It's amazing to see one give, and keep on giving when it seems like there is nothing more to give. Where are these extra resources, and endless energy coming from? It took me many years, and many life experiences to find the answer to this question. God has put my parents, grandparents, godmother and countless other people in my life to help me come to this point of understanding today. This knowledge has opened a door to many of life's mysteries. I now understand that it is better to give than to receive. I now fully understand that love, joy, happiness, contentment, peace of mind, and a reasonable portion of health are priceless. I understand that we serve God by serving others. I understand that God can make a way out of no way. I understand that even when I am by myself, that I am never truly alone. I understand that just as others have encouraged me, helped me, prayed with me, and for me along this life's journey; I must do the same for others.

My parents, grandparents, and godmother are not here, but their acts and words of wisdom are embedded in me. I do for others with no desire or expectation of anything in return. I've used my very last to help others in need, believing that God will make away out of no way. I've ministered to the sick when I was recovering from radiation treatment myself. Remembering how Mom; regardless of her health, cared for the sick in our community. Thinking of all of this gave me endless energy to be the helping hands for others. Remembering how Dad would pray over bags of grocery that they would be more than enough for our family; believing if it's God's will a little over for others if needed. I was inspired when I saw Dad walk around his garden talking to God for a plentiful harvest. I was also inspired being with Dad as he introduced others to the life of Jesus Christ. What a great way to serve God by using one's life as an example to show it is better to give than to receive. I believe that it was God's plan to put me in this family to experience, appreciate and be an active part of his plan. I see myself as one of the countless others used as helping hands.

There were so many things I didn't understand as a child. I even felt like Mom and Dad over reacted on some issues. Now I find myself doing some of the same things. Only now I understand my feelings, and why there are certain things I must do for my family. At night I feel that it is a must that I pray over my children, and just touch them. I just have to thank God for them, and ask for his continued blessings and protection of them. I cook balanced meals that taste good and good for them. There isn't a rule that says healthy foods should taste bad; so I just make healthy foods that taste good. I taught my kids skills for life by making games out of almost every life situation. The teacher in me made me post notes all over the house. Mom and Dad didn't post notes; they just gave us a verbal list, and believe me we followed the list.. Now I know that over reaction was really devotion of love and giving of quality time. My parents just wanted the best for us, and they wanted us to do our best as we traveled through life. My daughter gave me one of the best compliments without knowing it. Nena said, "Mom I find myself doing things just like you. Some days I feel like a young version of you. Is this normal"? After telling her I once had the same feelings about my mom. We both just had to laugh. Life is funny.

Our lives live on in our children, grandchildren, relatives, friends and even the people we meet as we travel this life's journey. Each day is so perfectly planned. Each choice made determines where we will be, and what we will be doing at any given time. Since no day can be repeated, it's important to make the best of each day, help others along the way, and if need be helped by others. I must say that God has created a perfect world, and a perfect plan to care for every living thing within it. What a joy it is to let God use us to carry out his plan. As we serve others we serve God.

My parents showed me God's love by being his hands on earth to give, and care for others unconditionally. They have been willing to cloth, feed, open their home, as well as introduce others to this life of Jesus Christ. What a great way to serve God; by being an example and a testimony.

A TALK WITH GOD
THANK YOU FOR CHOOSING ME

Chapter 10

Dear God;

Our Father, which art in heaven; it's once more, and again that I call upon your precious name. Dear Father, as I look back on my life I just have to say "Thank You". There are a lot of things that I don't understand, nor do I understand the reason for them. Father I do believe that you have allowed people and situations, or experiences as you might call them; to protect and guide me throughout my life.

Of all the marvelous beings you've made, you chose me to live this life. Again, I must say "Thank You". You've blessed me so much and you're still blessing me now. Some people are thankful for one "good" parent; Father you blessed me two "good" parents. You allowed me to grow up in a loving Christian home. You brought me through medical situations that could have taken my life; but you saw fit to bring me through. When I asked for another child, you gave it to me. Not by my time table, but years later by yours; just a few days before my fortieth birthday. As a teacher and mentor, you've given me a chance to touch many lives. You've given me the opportunity to care for the homeless, feed the hungry, cloth the needy, care for the sick and shut-in. Father I thank you for letting me be on the giving end, and not on the receiving end. Dear Father, thank you.

Father you've given me a Christian husband and three healthy children. Thank you for letting me return home for Daddy's home going. And Dear Father, I thank you for letting me take part in Mama's home going. It was a beautiful experience for Mama's four girls to surround her bed as she slowly and peacefully slept away. Oh Gracious God I do thank you.

Father, you know I don't ask a lot for myself, but Father today I am. Father continue to bless me with knowledge, health, and wisdom to continue to touch and bless the lives of others. Father I thank you for blessing my two older children with successful careers. But Father, most of all let me live to see Dontaye become a strong Christian man. Father if it's your will, please let me see Dontaye graduate from college, or receive a trade or business that will help him reach his financial goal. Father it would really be nice to see all my grandchildren.

Father I know this has been a long talk, but I just had so much to say. I ask all these blessing in the precious name of Your Son, Jesus Christ.

Amen.

CITATIONS

Davis, Dernoral; Feature Story; <u>When Youth Protest: The Mississippi Civil Rights Movement,1955- 1970</u>; Mississippi History Now, MS Historical Society; 2000

Dreher, Arielle; <u>How Integration Failed in Jackson's Public Schools from 1969 to 2017</u>; Jackson Free Press; November 15, 2017.

Jackson State University; <u>The May 1970 Tragedy at Jackson State University</u>; May 1070.

Kent State University Libraries; <u>Special Collections and Archives-Chronology of Events;</u> May 1-4, 1970

Sorrels, James E.; <u>The Pearl River Valley Reservoir Project,</u> Bureau of Governmental Research; The University of Mississippi, 1962

The Angling Channel; FLW Mississippi Division @ Ross Barnett Reservoir, MS; March 18, 2017.

The Clarion Ledger Jackson, MS local; <u>Central High School Jackson, MS</u>; June, 1969

Wolf, Paul; Cover Photo; <u>Smith Robertson Museum and Cultural Center of Jackson, MS.;</u> MY CITY JXN.MS; oct 19, 2020.

Chronological News Reporting:

WLBT (NBC); spring 1963

WAPT (ABC); spring 1963

WJTV (CBS); spring 1963

WJTV (CBS); August 28-30, 1963

Sam M. Brinkley High School Intercom announcement; November 22, 1963.

WJTV (CBS); November 22, 1963

WJTV (CBS); July 2-4, 1964

WJTV (CBS); June 26-28, 1966

WJTV (CBS); April 4, 1968